Concepts and Persons

THE TANNER LECTURES
ON HUMAN VALUES

Concepts and Persons

THE TANNER LECTURES
ON HUMAN VALUES

Michael Lambek

with Commentary by

Jonathan Lear

Sherry B. Ortner

Joel Robbins

UNIVERSITY OF TORONTO PRESS

Toronto   Buffalo   London

ISBN 978-1-4875-0905-7 (cloth)
ISBN 978-1-4875-3959-7 (PDF)
ISBN 978-1-4875-3960-3 (EPUB)

Library and Archives Canada Cataloguing in Publication

Title: Concepts and persons / Michael Lambek ; with commentary by
    Jonathan Lear, Sherry Ortner, Joel Robbins.
Names: Lambek, Michael, author.
Series: Tanner lectures on human values (Cambridge, Mass.)
Description: Series statement: The Tanner lectures on human
    values | Includes bibliographical references and index.
Identifiers: Canadiana (print) 20210214945 | Canadiana (ebook)
    20210215054 | ISBN 9781487509057 (cloth) | ISBN 9781487539597 (PDF) |
    ISBN 9781487539603 (EPUB)
Subjects: LCSH: Philosophical anthropology.
Classification: LCC BD450 .L24 2021 | DDC 128 – dc23

Title page image: Barbara Hepworth © Bowness. Photograph courtesy of
The Pier Arts Centre.

University of Toronto Press acknowledges the financial assistance to its
publishing program of the Canada Council for the Arts and the Ontario
Arts Council, an agency of the Government of Ontario.

Canada Council   Conseil des Arts
for the Arts   du Canada

ONTARIO ARTS COUNCIL
CONSEIL DES ARTS DE L'ONTARIO
an Ontario government agency
un organisme du gouvernement de l'Ontario

Funded by the   Financé par le
Government   gouvernement
of Canada   du Canada

Canada

Contents

Foreword

John Dewey once said, "Philosophy recovers itself when it ceases to be a device for dealing with the problems of philosophers and becomes a method, cultivated by philosophers, for dealing with the problems of men."[1] Dewey urged philosophers to get out of their armchairs and start their philosophizing from the problems people encounter in their lives. To do this well requires that they engage those already in the field who have devised diverse ways of studying people and their problems. Those studying the human condition through other modes also invariably draw on normatively freighted ideas that pose questions and difficulties that are frequent subjects of philosophical investigation. We – philosophers and non-philosophers – would do well to think together in our attempts to make sense of, and cope with, our predicaments.

In this spirit, and in the spirit of the Tanner Lectures themselves, the Philosophy Department at University of Michigan has long stressed the importance of inviting people from fields outside philosophy – including biology, classics, economics, history, law, literature, psychiatry, psychology, and sociology – to deliver the annual Tanner Lecture on Human Values. When, as chair of the Philosophy Department, I had occasion to invite the next Tanner lecturer, I noticed that the last anthropologist we had invited was Marshall Sahlins, in 2005. Since then, anthropology has turned ever more seriously to ethical dimensions of life – to the fact that people understand and deal with their condition not simply in terms of challenges to the

---

1   Dewey, "The Need for a Recovery of Philosophy (1917)," in *The Essential Dewey*, vol. 1, 68.

satisfaction of their desires or the advancement of their interests but in ethical terms – as, for example, duties to fulfil, sins to avoid, and ideals to realize. I was therefore delighted to invite Michael Lambek, Professor and Canada Research Chair in the Anthropology of Ethical Life at the University of Toronto – and, as his title indicates, a leader in the anthropology of ethics – to deliver our 2019 Tanner Lecture.

Lambek draws on the work of several philosophers – including Stanley Cavell, Cora Diamond, Jonathan Lear, Alasdair MacIntyre, Gilbert Ryle, and Ludwig Wittgenstein – to explore the predicaments that arise in the ways people live with concepts, and with persons. He is particularly concerned with our ambiguous relations to "metapersons" – spirits, deities, demons, saints, and other human-like figures. It is far too easy to dismiss metapersons as unreal, and hence as concepts we should live without. Even atheists often relate to metapersons in fiction, drama, and history, and to currently existing humans reconfigured in our culture as metapersons – for example, pop-music idols and pro-wrestling personas. We fantasize about them, heroize and demonize them, write fanfiction about them, engage in cosplay. Concerns about their ontological status are often orthogonal to the varied ways engaging with metapersons animate ethical life.

While Lambek warns that it is too "heavy handed ... to describe metahumans as the anthropomorphization of concepts," that is not a bad starting place for considering one way we engage with them. Ethical concepts are often better contended with when we imagine how particular metapersons manifest them in particular circumstances than in the abstractions of philosophical analysis. When Christians ask, "What would Jesus do?"; when Hillary Clinton imagined conversing with Eleanor Roosevelt to help her think about how to face challenges in her life; or when audience members at a performance of Tennessee Williams's *Cat on a Hot Tin Roof* reflect on Brick's alcoholism to make sense of the addiction of one of their own family members, they engage with metapersons as guides to action and understanding.

Sometimes metapersons trouble us. We may feel haunted by ancestors with whom we had fraught relations – unforgiven wrongs, buried secrets, failures to communicate. Lambek seeks to illuminate the human condition by focusing on the case of Salim, a young man from Mayotte who is haunted not only by unfinished business with his suddenly deceased mother but by the spirits with whom his mother, a professional spirit-handler, engaged. The latter hound him in his dreams, demanding to strike up a relationship with him in accordance with their practice, upon the death of their handlers, of seeking cohabitation with the deceased's descendants. As a reformed Muslim, he regards them all as devils with whom it is sinful to interact, even if only to ask them to go away. One can be a good Muslim, or interact with spirits, but not both. Salim is also overcome with guilt at his failure to warn his mother against engaging with spirits, as doing so would send her to hell. Other Muslims in Mayotte have more easy-going relationships with various spirits, as longstanding local customs hold that only some are evil. Embracing a both/and perspective on the concepts informing their ethical lives, they see no conflict between being a good Muslim and engaging with spirits.

Lambek argues that Salim's troubles exemplify a type of ethical conflict that may arise for *any* persons whose lives are informed by incommensurable ethical concepts. Since nearly all of us inhabit societies that include multiple incommensurable ethical traditions informing our lives, Salim's troubles offer materials for reflection about our own. In Salim's case, the reformed Muslim concept of "devil" is incommensurable with the diverse concepts of spirits in local Mayotte culture. Lambek argues that, in regarding the latter as all devils and hence as commensurable with reformed Islamic notions, Salim makes a conceptual mistake. If we understand the meanings of concepts through their roles in language games – in how we live with them – we can understand Salim as taking a concept of spirits belonging to one language game and treating it according to the rules of another. Although he feels compelled to live strictly in accordance with reformed Islam and hence to repudiate traditional ways with spirits, he cannot repudiate the latter without experiencing turmoil – in part because repudiation also puts him in seemingly unresolvable tension with his deceased mother.[2]

---

2 It is as if, in the midst of an American football game, Salim catches the ball and starts playing with it according to the rules of rugby. Although he is dedicated to playing rugby exclusively, Salim finds that he cannot simply ignore the consequences of finding himself in a football game.

As with all rich explorations of the human condition, Lambek's lecture raises more questions than it answers. His commentators ask many of them. Sherry Ortner, Distinguished Professor of Anthropology at UCLA, asks what more can be learned about Salim's predicaments, and our own, by further pursuing the metaphor of social life as a set of games. Jonathan Lear, John U. Nef Distinguished Service Professor at the Committee on Social Thought and Professor of Philosophy at the University of Chicago, asks how we might view Salim's troubles, and hence our own, by incorporating psychoanalytic, temporal, and developmental perspectives on his distress – considering how he may be misled by "motivated self-misunderstanding," how his interactions with Lambek might be a creative way for him to work through his mourning, and how taking an ironic perspective on the divergent expectations of the different traditions that inform his life might enable him to live well "with apparent contradictions." Joel Robbins, Sigrid Rausing Professor of Social Anthropology at the University of Cambridge, asks how we might better appreciate the merits of a life lived by an either/or logic such as Salim's, which insists on subsuming plural traditions under the ethical framework of a dominant one, in comparison to the life lived by a both/and logic, such as that of other denizens of Mayotte who accept both Islam and relations with spirits, and of anthropologists themselves.

It may be the case, as Lambek suggests, that making conceptual mistakes is inherent in the human condition, whether we live by a both/and or an either/or logic. If so, we need to ask the ethical question of how to live with such mistakes. Lambek's reflections illuminate the diverse challenges we face in answering this question.

Elizabeth Anderson
John Dewey Distinguished
University Professor of Philosophy
and Women's Studies,
University of Michigan, Ann Arbor

Preface and Acknowledgments

The Tanner Lecture was delivered at the invitation of the Department of Philosophy, University of Michigan, on 30 January 2019 and was followed the next day by a symposium with three respondents and my response to their commentaries, all prepared in advance. Although the lecture had been scheduled a year earlier, that January day in 2019 found Ann Arbor, like much of the Midwest, caught in a polar vortex. The frigid conditions made travel to the city difficult. Moreover, the university shut down most of its operations and relocated the lecture at the last minute to a hotel, where, unfortunately, it could not be recorded. The event nevertheless drew a significant and hardy audience.

What follows is a verbatim copy of the text that the respondents received, and most of which the audience heard. The lecture itself is published first in *The Tanner Lectures on Human Values,* Volume 38 (Salt Lake City: The University of Utah Press, 2020), and is reprinted here with the permission of the University of Utah Press. Since the respondents' comments are also being published as they were written, and here for the first time, I have agreed not to alter the text of the original lecture. Despite the long delay, the lecture stands as it was originally sent to the respondents in October 2018. The comments of the respondents follow the lecture, in the order in which I received them in January 2019. They are each respectively followed by my responses, now somewhat expanded from the form in which they were delivered in Ann Arbor. Brief additional thoughts come at the end of my responses to the individual commentaries.

Because I had a lot to say, and only an hour to say it, a number of ideas found their way into the notes. As the lecture grew, sentences originally in the main text found themselves pushed to the notes.

The present version has been designed so that the notes can be read alongside the main text. Early readers report that it is easiest to read the text once through without the notes and a second time with them.

I owe deep debts of gratitude to many people: first and foremost, to the endowers of the Tanner Lectures; to Elizabeth Anderson and the Department of Philosophy at the University of Michigan for the invitation and for Professor Anderson's thoughtful foreword; and to Andrew Shryock and the Department of Anthropology at Michigan for their support. I thank Mark Schlissel, President of the University of Michigan, for his opening remarks and am especially grateful to him and all the audience members for braving the cold.

A number of readers have improved the text. Cheryl Misak provided a courageous reading of the initial draft that instigated major changes in exposition. Paul Antze, Janice Boddy, Veena Das, Michael Jackson, and especially Jack Sidnell offered comments on later drafts. Juliet Floyd provided critical instruction on a point of Wittgenstein. Nadia Lambek, Simon Lambek, and Jackie Solway said the right things at critical moments.

I was very lucky in Elizabeth's selection of interlocutors. I am deeply indebted to Jonathan Lear, Sherry Ortner, and Joel Robbins, who took the time not only to engage with my thinking but to travel to Ann Arbor in the dead of winter and despite the impediments caused by the weather. They are true colleagues. While in Ann Arbor I referred to them each by first name, I have revised the text here to use last names.

I received many helpful responses to the lecture and the following symposium, especially from Sarah Buss, Allan Gibbard, Webb Keane, Michael Lempert, and Eric Swanson. Webb also chaired the symposium, deploying his usual wit. Cora Diamond graciously responded to an email from a complete stranger with a generous reading of the lecture after the fact. Sandra Bamford added a useful suggestion, and a group of graduate students and postdoctoral fellows participated in a fruitful seminar on the original text. My editor at the University of Toronto Press, Jodi Lewchuk, enthusiastically made my project hers as well. Debbie Durham ably created the index and Lisa Jemison saw the book through production.

I owe a great debt to the people in Mayotte who guided me in understanding their world and lives, especially here the man I call Salim. Successive research grants from the Social Sciences and Humanities Research Council of Canada supported fieldwork, while a Canada Research Chair helped provide time to think and write.

I had the particular good fortune to deliver the Tanner Lecture at the institution where, forty years earlier, I completed my doctorate. I dedicate the lecture to the memory of two exceptional mentors at Michigan, Aram Yengoyan and Skip (Roy) Rappaport. And I salute a third mentor, Henry Wright, and a fellow graduate student, Susan Wineberg, whose presence at the lecture were signs of enduring friendship.

Concepts and Persons:
The Tanner Lecture

All problems pertaining to humankind are ultimately problems for humankind.

Claude Lévi-Strauss, "Anthropology and the 'Truth Sciences'"[1]

Broadly speaking, anthropologists divide according to whether they conceive their subject as the human condition, what humans *face* and what we *do*, or as human nature, what we *are*. Having pitched my tent in the former camp, and taking the occasion as one for speaking boldly, I pick up the old idea that a good way to approach the human condition is by means of distinctions humans cannot overcome, including the one I have just made between existence and essence. My subject concerns what Veena Das has recently called the "struggle to make living and thinking commensurable to each other."[2] I will follow a course between arguing for the prevalence in our thinking of conceptual mistakes and diagnosing a specific instance and its effects on a life, a kind of ethnographic case history.

As an anthropologist speaking at the invitation of philosophers, I will say – and inevitably show – something about the relationship between our respective fields. This question is currently in vogue, and it deserves not a definitive answer or division of labour but depiction as a conversation between friends or perhaps a Cavellian

---

1   Lévi-Strauss, "Anthropology and the 'Truth Sciences,'" 247.
2   Das, "The Life of Concepts," 319. See also Das, "What Does Ordinary Ethics Look Like?"

comedy of remarriage.[3] I hope that my rapid pace and eclectic citation practices, so different from philosophy's deliberate mode of procedure, will not prove too infuriating. (The qualifications are in the notes.) It will be evident that anthropologists, at least this one, still have much to learn from philosophy, but I take the occasion also to afford a gesture in the other direction. Whatever the outcome, it is an invitation I am very honoured and humbled to receive.

1 Anthropology under Description

Whereas some philosophers see their task as a therapeutic one of uncovering and possibly redressing mistakes of reason, anthropologists have taken the converse path of showing that systems of thought and practice in societies that the West has dominated and

---

3 From the anthropologists' side, see for example Das, Jackson, Kleinman, and Singh, eds, *The Ground Between: Anthropologists Engage Philosophy*. Jackson has for years woven connections with phenomenology and existentialism; see, inter alia, Jackson, *Minima Ethnographica*; and Jackson, *Existential Anthropology*. Das is informed by Wittgenstein and Cavell in *Life and Words* and elsewhere. For (post)structuralist and Deleuzian provocations, see, for example, Eduardo Viveiros de Castro, "The Relative Native." See (anthropologist) Cheryl Mattingly and (philosopher) Thomas Schwarz Wentzer, "Toward a New Humanism," for the argument that the link between the respective disciplines affords the opportunity to speak productively again about the human. In part this is in response to the recent fashion concerning the "posthuman," many of whose insights can be found in what was once called ecological anthropology; for the less reductionist versions, see Bateson, *Steps to an Ecology of Mind*; and Rappaport, *Ritual and Religion in the Making of Humanity*. Where Thomas Kuhn, *The Structure of Scientific Revolutions*, describes incommensurability between *successive* paradigms, Gilbert Ryle in his 1953 Tarner Lectures, *Dilemmas*, speaks of what he calls discrepancies and dilemmas between the vocabularies of *contemporaneous* disciplines or practices and between technical discourse and ordinary speech. Anthropology and philosophy do not map onto distinct natural entities or divide the world in a clear-cut fashion. One can live with either or both without worrying too much about the boundaries between them. In fact, worrying too much about the boundaries would be to live badly with them.

defined itself against are no less rational, acute, or ethically fine-tuned than our ideals of ourselves.[4] To encounter meaning, order, reason, beauty, and eudaimonia in remote and distinctive worlds is what once inspired anthropologists of my kind. But this meant not fully attending to the ways people living in such worlds may be as subject to dilemma, debate, uncertainty, error, and ethical impasse as the rest of us. These matters are certainly exacerbated by the conquest, inequality, exploitation, subjection, and precarity that have become the more central concerns of anthropology, but they are not to be reduced or limited to them.[5]

Phrased more positively and less judgmentally, anthropologists explore the ways and means by which people interpret their lives, culture, and circumstances in the course of living them,[6] and how, in effect, they articulate, draw upon, are vulnerable to, and sometimes mistake or lose their concepts.[7] As a general description,

---

4 Hence if philosophy is an activity to clarify our thinking, anthropology is never that of clarifying the thinking of others *to them*. On rationality see, famously, Evans-Pritchard, *Witchcraft, Oracles and Magic among the Azande*, but also *The Nuer* on social ascription; Lévi-Strauss, *The Savage Mind* (*La Pensée Sauvage*); Douglas, *Purity and Danger*; Tambiah, *Culture, Thought, and Social Action*, and also the so-called rationality debate (Hollis and Lukes, eds, *Rationality and Relativism*). Wittgenstein, *Remarks on Frazer's Golden Bough*, is an intervention that inspires anthropologists, as the newly translated edition and commentaries (Palmié and da Col, eds and trans., *The Mythology in Our Language: Remarks on Frazer's Golden Bough*) shows.

5 See, from a vast literature, Farmer, "Never Again? Reflections on Human Values and Human Rights"; Stoler, *Duress*; and Ortner, "Dark Anthropology and Its Others." Whereas precarity, injustice, and exploitation are subjects proper to anthropology, they are by no means what distinguishes the field from others.

6 In this usage, "interpretation" is active and not merely reflective, the living and not merely the gloss on it. I have compared the interpretation of culture (i.e., of available texts, models, etc.) to the way musicians interpret a score or directors and actors interpret a script (Lambek, "The Interpretation of Lives or Life as Interpretation"). Each interpretation is unique, and together they lay the sediment that builds a tradition, much as successive interpretations of Socrates and Plato, and interpretations of those interpretations, have produced the tradition called (Western) philosophy.

7 Diamond, "Losing Your Concepts." Das, "What Does Ordinary Ethics Look Like?," provides a deep account of living with concepts. Lear, *Radical Hope*, offers a picture of losing not merely concepts but an entire world.

living with concepts suggests a less rigid mode of existence than one of adhering to rules, holding beliefs, acceding to norms, or subjecting to discipline. It depicts acts and conversations, investments in given and new concepts and modes of practice or play, and the embrace of ambiguity, imagination, and experiment,[8] albeit within certain structures and constraints, notably of grammar, power, and authority. Living with concepts is not to be identified with, or reduced to, applying rules of logic or evidence.[9]

What *anthropologists* do is also sometimes described as interpreting, here not in the sense of enactment but of reading metaphorical texts. This is a practice in which I have been much invested; but increasingly I find it an insufficient description of what I do. To consider "meaningful action as text," as Paul Ricoeur once so helpfully guided me,[10] is to look away from action itself. What anthropologists observe and talk about with interlocutors are not disembodied meanings but meaningful *acts*. What I attend to is people putting things under description, and I too then put them under further description. As Elizabeth Anscombe demonstrated, any given act can be put under multiple descriptions, or, one could say, under concepts. And it follows from John Austin that putting something under description is itself an act or, conversely, that what constitutes something *as* an act is putting it under description.[11] That is something people do, put their acts and circumstances under description, debate what the better (more accurate,

---

8 Mattingly, *Moral Laboratories*.

9 One might speak comprehensively of the art, or arts, of living, a phrase I take from Nehamas, *The Art of Living*. I cannot here develop a comparison with the related concepts of practice (Ortner, *Anthropology and Social Theory*) and practices (MacIntyre, *After Virtue*).

10 Ricoeur, "The Model of the Text"; Lambek, *Human Spirits*.

11 Anscombe, *Intention*, esp. 37–47; Austin, *How to Do Things with Words*. That putting under descriptions is putting under concepts is an observation I owe to Cheryl Misak (personal communication). However, as Jack Sidnell suggests (personal communication), concepts and descriptions are not the same, insofar as, with respect to descriptions, we imply that we are talking about alternative ways of speaking about the same thing, whereas with concepts we imply that we are speaking about different things.

relevant, etc.) criteria and descriptions are in the circumstances, and either live according to the descriptions under which they have put themselves or find themselves put, or challenge given descriptions, establish new ones, and evaluate their practice accordingly.[12] These are central features of our lives with concepts, and they transcend individual concerns with meaning; performatively established descriptions objectify social reality.[13]

I am proposing a description of something I do as recording the acts of people putting things under description, debating their descriptions, living under them, and sometimes trying to escape them. I try to hear what the descriptions are, understand the judgment made in placing them, discern the authority by which certain descriptions prevail, explore the order or incommensurability among the descriptions locally available, and finally, put all this under further descriptions that draw from or constitute the conceptual vocabulary of anthropology.[14] This vocabulary derives

12 Some of what we put under description originates as expression; I am not proposing an argument of description as against expression (cf Gibbard, *Wise Choices, Apt Feelings*). On the relation of (discontinuous) acts or performances to (ongoing) practice see Lambek, *The Ethical Condition*, chapter 11. Cora Diamond adds that, "Any moral psychology is incomplete if it leaves out the ways imagination enters acts (and thoughts and talk) and the understanding of those acts (and thoughts and talk)" ("The Importance of Being Human," 41).

13 This statement draws from arguments in Rappaport, *Ritual and Religion*; and Berger and Luckmann, *The Social Construction of Reality*. It is also congruent with certain ideas of Judith Butler and Ian Hacking.

14 Of course, philosophy too could be said to describe. At least, that was Wittgenstein's later view in rejecting the alternatives of theorizing or explaining. "What Wittgenstein means when he says that philosophy really is descriptive is that it is descriptive of 'our grammar,' of 'the criteria we have' in understanding one another, knowing the world" (Cavell, "The Availability of Wittgenstein's Later Philosophy," 56). To put under description or to observe people putting their actions under description is a matter of discerning or determining what language game is at issue; but equally, different language games on the part of the thinker lead to different kinds of "description," and it is unlikely that those of philosophy and anthropology will be identical. Ryle explores the significance of differences between the descriptions of various kinds of experts and those

from and further develops a history of comparison of concepts and practices taken from the ethnography of multiple societies but also from social theory and the archive of concepts and arguments that is called philosophy, as I have just borrowed "putting under a description." I look to philosophy for better descriptions of what people do and what I do myself.[15]

What in turn can anthropology offer philosophy? Not only does it report on foreign concepts, descriptions, arguments, theories, even entire traditions, challenging philosophy to broaden its horizons and expand the range of its conversation and examples,[16] and not only does it show people thinking and acting in contexts that

---

of ordinary knowledge, such that the painter of scenery "is not doing bad geology and the geologist is not doing good or bad landscape painting" (*Dilemmas*, 80). "The nuclear physicist, the theologian, the historian, the lyric poet and the man in the street produce very different, yet compatible and even complementary pictures of one and the same 'world.'" Yet Ryle cautions that the analogy is perilous because "the highly concrete word 'picture' smothers the enormous differences between the business of the scientist, historian, poet and theologian … Indeed, this smothering effect of using notions like depicting, describing, explaining, and others to cover highly disparate things reinforces other tendencies to assimilate the dissimilar and unsuspiciously to impute just those parities of reasoning, the unreality of which engenders dilemmas" (81). Ryle, of course, famously supplied Clifford Geertz with the concept of "thick description." *That* concept is presupposed but not explicitly addressed in this lecture (Geertz, "Thick Description," citing Ryle, "Thinking and Reflecting" and "The Thinking of Thoughts," in Ryle, *Collected Papers, Vol. 2*).

15 As Richard Bernstein puts it, "The task is always to find the resources within our own horizon, linguistic practices, and experience that can enable us to understand what confronts us as alien" (*Beyond Objectivism and Relativism*, 173). Concepts I have borrowed from philosophy include phronesis, incommensurability, horizon, and illocutionary acts.

16 Here one must acknowledge alternative traditions of philosophy, such as those characteristic of East and South Asia, and also anthropological accounts of philosophizing, from Radin, *Primitive Man as Philosopher*, through recent work like that of Kresse, *Philosophizing in Mombasa*, as well as work that understands cultural and linguistic practices as insightful in a manner comparable to philosophy (e.g., Witherspoon, *Language and Art in the Navajo Universe*; and Werbner, *Divination's Grasp*). Another approach has been to draw on foreign concepts and practices to parochialize our own; a significant intervention here is Mahmood, *Politics of Piety*.

differ in terms of language, tradition, opportunities, constraints, and projects from what philosophers generally encounter and possibly take for granted, but it can show philosophy the relevance or limits of its own concepts as anthropologists apply them to new contexts or in different projects, as I do here.

Some have argued that anthropology complements the abstract thought and hypothetical or literary examples of philosophy with the lived, practical, real world, that is, with context itself. In a catchy slogan, Tim Ingold has called anthropology "philosophy with the people in."[17] This is condescending – implying that anthropology is philosophy enriched; misleading – insofar as much anthropology leaves people out and philosophy is full of people, not least other philosophers whom you cite or argue with; and empty, if it doesn't say what philosophy *is*. Nevertheless, perhaps the relation between concepts and persons differs in our respective fields.[18] It is the relation of concepts and persons in ordinary life that I explore.

---

17 Ingold, "Editorial." Here is the full text: "Philosophers, of course, have speculated on [the human] predicament for centuries, and might even claim such activity as their special preserve. Rarely if ever, however, do they enlist the help of ordinary people in their enterprise, or test their insights against the wisdom of common sense. Anthropology is a kind of philosophy too, but it is not so exclusive. There are, of course, as many definitions of anthropology as there are anthropologists, but my own is as follows: *Anthropology is philosophy with the people in,*" 696 (emphasis in original). From a review of previous Tanner Lectures, it is evident that the human has often been indistinguishable from Euro-American inheritors of classical and biblical traditions. Here I follow one of the missions of anthropology, which is to bring in other voices, less "philosophy with the people in" than philosophy with *other* people in.

18 "For many [philosophers], philosophy is essentially the a priori analysis of concepts, which can and should be done without leaving the proverbial armchair" (Margolis and Laurence, "Concepts"). For anthropologists, "people" indicates the social: people always in relation to other people and always in relation to structures, norms, and descriptions already in place. People are always already shaped by prior thoughts, actions, relations, power, and circumstances. The "anthropological" person is neither free nor determined but underdetermined (Lambek, *The Ethical Condition*). These descriptions are not meant to discount the range of things

The kind of anthropology I practise does build from direct encounters with people.[19] I introduce two orders of persons I have encountered in the course of fieldwork in Mayotte, an island in the Comoro Archipelago in the western Indian Ocean. First are villagers who practise Islam and speak Kibushy, a dialect of Malagasy.[20] Mayotte is not the ideal autonomous society that has served as the main locus for anthropological thought about thought but a heterogeneous place forged through regional movements shaped by trade, plantation capitalism, and colonialism. Over the past forty years, inhabitants have participated in rapid change, abandoning subsistence cultivation, acquiring access to Western education and health care, and becoming, since 2011, full citizens of France and the EU. I have visited the same community eleven times between 1975 and 2015.[21]

The second order of persons I call metapersons or metahumans, terms recently suggested by Marshall Sahlins for figures more or less than human, including spirits, deities, and demons.[22] They are often assigned to "religion," a concept I will try, not entirely successfully, to avoid.[23] Diverse among themselves, metahumans are

---

philosophers and anthropologists do, including the diversity of ways they describe, dispute, and justify them.

19 I do not claim it meets Austin's aspiration for "fieldwork in philosophy" (Austin, "A Plea for Excuses," 183). See also Moody-Adams, *Fieldwork in Familiar Places*. It is by no means obvious that anthropologists and philosophers mean the same thing by "fieldwork." Moreover, philosophers are more likely to draw from literature. "Why not take examples from life?" asks Bernard Williams, *Shame and Necessity*, 13. Because, he answers, "what philosophers will lay before themselves and their readers as an alternative to literature will not be life, but bad literature" (ibid.).

20 Kibushy is secondary in Mayotte to Shimaore, a Bantu language close to Swahili. Malagasy is Austronesian. Both have many loan words from Arabic and French.

21 Lambek, *Island in the Stream*.

22 Sahlins, "The Original Political Society." Philippe Descola speaks of "incarnates" ("Presence, Attachment, Origin"). Godfrey Lienhardt in his superlative account of the Dinka of Southern Sudan (*Divinity and Experience*) refers to "powers." "Extra-human" might also be apposite.

23 Living and working with *that* concept is another story. See Lambek, "What Is 'Religion' for Anthropology?"

beings of different nature from humans, more or less powerful, and sharing certain qualities and degrees of human personhood.[24] Meta-humans live alongside humans in various degrees of proximity, mutuality, intimacy, interference, and indifference. They may be, as Lévi-Strauss suggested of dogs and birds respectively, metonymical or metaphorical humans, forming part of our lives or merely evoking them.[25] The various concepts of metahumans present in Mayotte are generally incommensurable with one another, such that I cannot discover or impose an elegant grid of classification. The tokens of some of these types function more or less as individuated persons.

Among the metahumans prevalent in Mayotte and in neighbouring Madagascar are those I have translated as "spirits" and described under the concept of "spirit possession." In local practice, spirits of several kinds periodically displace their hosts, speaking and acting in their stead. For many years, and from an external perspective, I have reflected on the affordances that speaking in more than one voice or as more than one person have for selfhood, social relations, historical consciousness, and for ethical life generally. Having followed the lives of a number of hosts and their families I have come to think that "cohabitation" is a better description than "possession" since episodes of altered consciousness form only pieces of broader relationships.[26] "Spirit" is also a problematic translation, but I have not found a less inadequate one.

In what follows I describe the difficulty one young man has to live with metahumans. I will then redescribe his situation as one

---

24 I have to leave aside the complex question of what constitutes personhood. For one argument, see Lambek, "The Continuous and Discontinuous Person."

25 Lévi-Strauss, *The Savage Mind*, 207. The French title *La Pensée Sauvage*, as is well known, is a pun on the wild in contrast to the domesticated pansy. Not only is *sauvage* mistranslated as "savage," but *pensée* inexplicably as "mind," a reified abstraction as far from the science of the concrete as one could get.

26 I have also been influenced by a different critique of the concept of "possession," as developed by Paul Christopher Johnson, "Toward an Atlantic Genealogy of Spirit Possession." See also my response: Lambek, "Afterword: Recognizing and Misrecognizing Spirit Possession."

of living with concepts. The wider aim is to consider human life as characterized by our relations with both persons and concepts and with the inevitable difficulties we face, or mistakes we make, with respect to each. This is not a simple comparison since persons and concepts are not of the same logical type. It also raises the question of how descriptions taken from a small island could speak to broader questions. To this I give an old answer.

In its two words "Human Values," the description of the Tanner Lectures summarizes both the subject and the central tension of anthropology – on the one hand, humanity, all of us, comprehensively and in our singularity as a species, and on the other, values in their diversity, distinctiveness, and relativity.[27] We cannot think of the one without the other.

The tension is condensed in the anthropological concept of culture that adverts at once to the human as a whole, Culture-with-a-capital-C, as at Michigan Leslie White taught it and as Yengoyan called it, and to distinctive formations. The puzzle stems from the fact that we are all alike, but all alike in being different, others to each other, and living in particular, if interconnected, worlds. The problem is formally similar to that between the concept of Mind and minds (other minds and one's own). We speak intelligibly, as Clifford Geertz, whose early formulations of the problem remain the best, put it, only when we speak in a particular language, not Language in the abstract.[28] What is universal to humans is investment in, and

27 By relativity of values I mean in the first instance nothing more than that any given value is scalar, a matter of degree. Elsewhere (Lambek, "Value and Virtue," chapter 10) I discuss the play between absolute and relative value, the problems of comparison, and the disquiet when values are subject to quantification, common measure, and ranking, a subject raised by Marx, Simmel, and many other thinkers. On value hierarchy, see Robbins, "Monism, Pluralism and the Structure of Value Relations," and "Dumont's Hierarchical Dynamism."

28 Geertz, "The Impact of the Concept of Culture on the Concept of Man"; see also Geertz, "The Growth of Culture and the Evolution of Mind," for the argument that culture and the brain co-evolved and hence are dependent on each other. This is compatible with a concept of natural history in Wittgenstein's sense in that it is "natural" while at the same time not reducible to the "biological." A general problem in anthropology is that

dependence on, particulars, acting with respect to given sets of criteria and under specific descriptions. This includes continuously expanding our horizons of understanding, as Gadamer describes, and equally, as Lévi-Strauss observed, continuously producing difference.[29] Geertz almost concludes, as I assert now, that the relationship of the particular to the universal has been misconstrued in much the way Gilbert Ryle argued that the dominant mode of understanding the relationship of mind and body is based on category mistakes.[30] Cultural universals and particulars cannot simply be added together or peeled apart because they are different aspects or logical types.

Despite various attempts to resolve the puzzles associated with the concept of culture, including pre-emptive attempts to define or dismiss it, we could simply say that anthropologists *live* with it.[31] It is an instance of living with a concept.

---

we often do not take the deepest thoughts of our practitioners seriously. Authors like Geertz or Jackson who have profound philosophical insight are briefly acknowledged but seldom built upon. In one respect this lecture is an attempt to recognize and develop lessons from Wittgenstein embedded in Geertz.

29 Gadamer, *Truth and Method*; Lévi-Strauss, *The Savage Mind*. In other words, cultural worlds are not closed to one another and respond both by expanding mutual understanding and conversely by constituting themselves through differences with one another.

30 Ryle, *The Concept of Mind*. One could argue further, though I don't pursue it here, that culture is to nature as mind is to body. However, a significant implication of Geertz's argument is that the distinction between the particular and the universal is *not* coextensive with that between culture and nature.

31 As perhaps philosophers live with the concept of mind. Looking back to the mid-twentieth century use of "culture," Geertz says, "We were condemned, it seemed, to working with a logic and a language in which concept, cause, form, and outcome had the same name" ("Passage and Accident: A Life of Learning," 10–11). He goes on to speak of "semantic anxiety." Wittgenstein's concepts of language games and forms of life (*Philosophical Investigations*), and Ryle's of category mistakes (*The Concept of Mind*) are helpful in de-reifying both culture and mind. To trespass in a subject where I have no business, perhaps the tension between the *Tractatus* and the *Philosophical Investigations* could itself be described as manifesting the unresolvable pull between understanding the human

On another front, it is evident that plurality characterizes not only relations between so-called cultures but relations within them.[32] If it is human to orient ourselves with respect to particular values, we cannot hold or act on them all at once, in equal measure, or in full consistency. Inherent in the very concept of a value is the possibility of displacing it for another value.[33] And if *we* talk about sharing values with others, we imply that there are *other* others with whom we do *not* share those values. The pronoun "we" is ambiguous in English; in Malagasy there is both an inclusive and an exclusive first-person plural ("we" as "all of us" and "we" as opposed to "you" or "they") such that speakers must exercise judgment as to which to say when. Such judgment of address and reference illustrates the contextual contingency of shared values.[34] It illustrates as well an ethical dimension of concept use. Practically speaking, you should question my action each time I say "we" in this lecture.[35] The broader point is that human situations

---

condition through universals or essentials and particulars or practices, and the struggle over how not to state that relationship falsely (cf Cora Diamond, "Von Wright on Wittgenstein in Relation to His Times").

32 Indeed, if the differences between cultures are less than is sometimes claimed, the diversity within them is more pervasive than anthropologists have generally shown, raising the question of whether treating cultures as bounded units is a useful fiction and relative to historical context. Although Geertz is said to exaggerate the difference between cultures, in his Tanner Lecture at Michigan ("The Uses of Diversity," 1985), he pointed to the diversity within contemporary society: "Like nostalgia, diversity is not what it used to be" (264), and "we are living more and more in the midst of an enormous collage" (272).

33 I will not continue here on the concept of value, which has its own large literature, including an intersection between philosophy and economics (Anderson, *Value in Ethics and Economics*) and an anthropological approach embracing economic, ethical, and semiotic value (Graeber, *Toward an Anthropological Theory of Value*). See also Otto and Willerslev, eds, "Value as Theory."

34 Jack Sidnell (personal communication) suggests that the first-person exclusive is used only in reference, never in address.

35 "Human values" comprehend a vast range across humanity past and present. Most Tanner lectures have stuck to the Athens-Jerusalem axis or spoken in the name of humanity writ large, in which the scope of the "we" is implicit. Nowadays, some will say that I have no business speaking

are constituted by means of distinctive and shifting conjunctions of values, language games, concepts, relations, and persons.

2 Salim under His Own Description

Towards the end of my latest visit to Mayotte as I was chatting with an old friend, Vita, we were approached by an earnest young man, perhaps in his late twenties, who declared he had long wanted to meet me.[36] Salim, as he introduced himself, astonished me by switching from Kibushy to fluent and idiomatic English; this was the first and only full English conversation I have held in Mayotte. He told me English was his favourite subject in school and he had won a prize in it. He did his *bac* in literature[37] – another first for me to encounter – continued in the university recently established in Mayotte, and was doing a correspondence master's. He liked nineteenth-century French novelists and was a fan of Baudelaire, but his favourite author was Voltaire! He was also an observant Muslim.

Salim said he was trying to find a topic for his thesis, but teaching duties (in a middle school, *collège*) left him little time, and he might give up the degree. I suggested seeking a scholarship; he was evidently gifted. But his main problem, he volunteered, was

---

outside my tradition, and others will say that I cannot do so in any case; in their stark form, these are premises that anthropology was founded against, but they influence why I distinguish describing from representing. The matter is more complex than the terms in which it is commonly argued.

36 This took place in July 2015. One could call what follows an anecdote, which, as such, has become a trite way to open an ethnographic text. I describe it as a significant event or encounter. It is edited from my fieldnotes, which were written shortly after the conversation took place. Some parts are paraphrase.

37 The *bac* or baccalaureate is the advanced high-school-leaving degree and a prerequisite for university. Every other *bac* achieved by community members that I know of has been in technical or commercial subjects. Salim said he had never left the island because he saw that people who went to France ended up drinking and being in bad company and never finished their degrees.

not his studies. His mother had died recently, and it really shocked him, especially the manner of her death, in her sleep with no prior warning.[38] "My mother was my best friend," he said. "We would talk together about everything. Now I have no one."

I asked if he was married. "Divorced," he replied, "but that's a long story." After more talk about literature and music he returned to marriage and said he had been married twice – both within the last four months! On the first marriage he found himself changed; he became depressed and angry, didn't want to see his wife, or to sleep with her. After two or three weeks he sent her away. He was very upset and didn't understand it. He looked around and took a different wife. That marriage lasted less than twenty-four hours. He said he was not angry at the women but at himself. He said he felt completely stuck; he didn't know what to do.

Salim added that he was bothered by "devils and all their bullshit." The Qur'an says that devils are not to be trafficked with. They are evil; their goal is to bring people to hellfire (*mahamay*); they all serve their master Ibilis (Satan). They visited Salim in his sleep and troubled him, female devils especially. They wanted to have sex with him. In fact, what gave them pleasure was watching him masturbate. He told me all this directly, in English and without any obvious embarrassment. He used the word "devils" for what I translate as "spirits." As for "bullshit" and "masturbate," neither are concepts I had encountered in Mayotte.[39]

I suggested he was angry at his mother for dying so suddenly. But Salim repeated that he was angry at himself. His mother was an expert (*fundi*) at handling the devils and made considerable money from her practice; she built three houses and was independent. But

---

38 She was fine the night before. In the morning he got a call from his father that his mother wouldn't wake up. They had to force open the door, which was locked on the inside. He went and shook her. She was lying on her stomach, and when he finally managed to roll her over, he could see from her face that she was dead. "It was really a shock."

39 Salim cannot have sex outside marriage (*mañamatu*) because that is a sin; one has to marry (by Islam, *kufungia*) first, as he did. This injunction has been largely disregarded in Mayotte. See note 54. The women he married had doubtless been married before.

that will lead her to hellfire. He should have stopped her and he didn't. Since her death, he prayed a lot for her sins to be removed.

Salim was certain he understood the Qur'an on these matters[40] and that he needed to rid himself of the devils' influence. They were interested in him well before his mother died. When they rose in his mother they always said not to worry, that they are inheritance and pass from parent to child. His sister had acquired them. But they are evil and one must have nothing to do with them. They ask for a pact with you, but actually the spirit medium becomes their slave. There is nothing redeeming about them.

Salim said he used to drink and take drugs. One day he discovered God – he stopped those things and focused on the mosque. When I suggested taking things in moderation, he observed that one way devils work is to get you to do things in extremes – for example, instead of doing your ablutions (*kutawaza*) in three motions, you increase them to five. He repeated how important Islam was to him. At the beginning, after his mother died, he even thought to join the fighting in Iraq and end his life doing battle for Islam. Then he realized it was devils tempting him to excess. It is not Islamic to kill people. The fighters themselves are caught by devils.

Salim said he had spoken previously to Vita, an active curer like his mother, about having the devils removed. But Salim was unsure, concerned that treatment might result in their choosing to rise in him and establish permanent relationships. When Salim excused himself to go pray, Vita, who had not understood the conversation but knew the gist, told me the salient thing Salim had left out – namely that after his mother died, Salim burned the spirits' (*lulu, djinn*) clothing and equipment, including cash his mother had received from clients.[41] Salim called them *haram*. Vita wryly

---

40 Unlike most of his fellow citizens, he appears to understand the meaning from Arabic of the Qur'anic verses. However, the Qur'an is ambiguous on *djinn*; see MacDonald, Massé, Boratav, Nizami, and Voorhoeve, "Djinn," in *Encyclopaedia of Islam*, accessed 7 May 2018: https://referenceworks .brillonline.com/entries/encyclopaedia-of-islam-2/*-COM_0191.

41 He did this along with, and possibly at the instigation of, one of his mother's younger sisters. One person later told me the amount in question was 3,000 euros; another person said 800.

observed that while Salim could be treated, he wouldn't take on the case himself for fear that if the spirits rose, Salim might accuse him of having abetted their presence.

Salim recounted events that overwhelm his life. His distress concerns not only his mother's demise but that he never dissuaded her from giving up her work with the devils and, what he omitted from his otherwise frank narrative, that he is subject to their anger for having destroyed their possessions and treated them with disrespect. Another medium, sympathetic to Salim, later told me that Salim's mother used to speak indiscreetly about practising sorcery (*voriky*) with the help of the spirits (*lulu*). This gave Salim further reason to worry about her condition in the afterlife.[42]

Meeting Salim was an event of sheer serendipity, almost as exciting and unexpected as being invited to give this lecture. But it was followed by frustrations more typical of fieldwork: the realization of questions left unasked and the inability to find Salim again or to learn whether his situation has since improved. Paradoxically, I am making central to my argument someone I barely know.[43] We might think of the situation as analogous to understanding a character in fiction in that there are limits to what the writer tells us.

By contrast, I know Vita well, having met him in 1975 when we were both about the age that Salim was in 2015 and, like Salim, eagerly poised to embrace what our respective horizons offered.[44]

---

42 On sorcery see Lambek, *Knowledge and Practice in Mayotte,* and "On Sorcery: Life with the Concept."

43 This rubs against my ethnographic practice, which is one of revisiting and conversing with interlocutors multiple times, fully talking through their ideas, and also talking with their consociates. By bad luck, I had barely known Salim's mother. His father I had largely avoided as someone rather unpleasant and unhelpful; on this occasion he proved unable to add anything about Salim and his mother. I have been close to Salim's paternal great-grandmother, grandparents, great uncles, and several of his uncles, aunts, and cousins. I do not know Salim's siblings; his father bragged of sixteen children, with several different wives. The father was also distraught at his wife's death but took another wife, as custom advises widows and widowers to do.

44 "We, who share this striking thing – having a human life to lead – may make in imagination something of what it is to have a human life to lead;

Vita is a devotee of the *Mulidy*, a sufi genre of dance and song in honour of the Prophet; with his deep beautiful voice Vita became a reputed performer and teacher. Disdaining what he considered hypocritical displays of piety in the mosque, he channelled his energies through music. Beauty, says Elaine Scarry, "is life-saving (or life creating … or life-altering …),"[45] and I think that what Scarry calls its "plenitude" has been salvific for Vita, who was plagued by a series of ailments which he attributed to sorcery.[46] Vita also developed a second métier, as a reputed healer. He hosts a number of spirits (*djinn, lulu*) who often appear frightening to others but who engage in teasing banter with his wife, who herself became an active medium. Vita's delight in the world of the spirits made him a wonderful teacher as I accompanied him on plant-collecting tours, sat in on consultations, or listened to his imaginative accounts. Vita's devotion to the sacred *Mulidy* and captivation by the amoral spirits sat comfortably together, incommensurable rather than in conflict, much as I imagine Salim juxtaposes his study of French literature with his piety.

3 Further Describing Salim's Situation

Understanding is a matter not only of empathy or (literal) translation but of placing things under further description, finding better terms and criteria with which to do so, and discerning different levels of description (from pumping water to poisoning a household, as it were).[47] Conversely, it may require knowing when to

---

and this imaginative response we may see (and judge and learn from) in the doings and words and customs of those who share *having a human life to lead*. That perception may belong to the understanding we want of those words or actions or customs" (Diamond, "The Importance of Being Human," 43–4).

45 Scarry, "On Beauty and Being Just," 23.

46 Vita married into the village and, although his wife is a cross-cousin, he often felt slighted by his in-laws and not fully at home.

47 Anscombe, in *Intention*, writes of a man moving his arm, pumping water, filling a tank, and (whether intentionally or unintentionally) poisoning a

stop placing things under description, of recognizing when "There are, indeed, things that cannot be put into words."[48]

Salim could make a prime candidate for psychoanalysis, given the succinct manifestation of conflict and his forthrightness in describing it. However, rather than speculating on his inner life, I stay mainly with the situation in which he finds himself. I want to see this for what it is, at once personal and singular, culturally and historically shaped, and deeply human. Salim's situation exemplifies the inextricability of thought and judgment, intellectual and moral reasoning, or, as I describe it here, relations with concepts and persons. I begin with persons.

I recognize Salim as a man stricken at the sudden loss of his mother. His tragedy, one could say after Stanley Cavell,[49] lies in failure to acknowledge his mother's separateness, a separation made all the more evident in her sudden death. But equally, perhaps Cavell's picture does not anticipate the value of intersubjectivity found in places like Mayotte. Salim's tragedy is also that he fails to fully acknowledge his *connectedness* to his mother and to and through the spirits. The situation is doubly intractable because Salim has a foot in more than one world, one that advocates autonomy, the other relationality.

Salim's worlds overlap with mine. He speaks of Flaubert and rappers and difficulty writing a thesis. He grieves for his mother, is subject to guilt, shame, and ambivalence. And yet there are differences. He has read Voltaire and I have not. He is a devout Muslim and I am not. He attends to the concept of punishment in the

---

household. A theory of description subsumes the problem of reductionism. As William James remarked (as cited by Merton, "A Life of Learning," 19), "A Beethoven string-quartet is truly … a scraping of horses' tails on cats' bowels, and may be exhaustively described in such terms; but the application of this description in no way precludes the simultaneous applicability of an entirely different description."

48 Wittgenstein, *Tractatus Logico-Philosophicus*, 6.522, as cited by Monk, *Ludwig Wittgenstein*, 143. The thought continues, "*They make themselves manifest.*"

49 Separateness is a leitmotif in Cavell. See his readings of *King Lear* ("The Avoidance of Love") and of *Othello* (in *The Claim of Reason*, Part Four).

afterlife; he is vulnerable to devils and their bullshit; his world includes a mother who lived happily with spirits or devils and who may have practised sorcery.

Salim is evidently a man of dignity and sensibility, caught in a dilemma with no obvious resolution. His quarrel is not with his kin or fellows but with metahumans. We could say, as he himself does, that the conflict is with himself, except for the fact that the metahumans are real for Salim and accepted as such in his community. His self is more porous than he would wish, and he is accountable not only to his mother but to the obligations she had with the spirits.

Salim lived in intimacy with his mother; she was his "best friend." Yet her death forces him to confront the fact that he had not sufficiently acknowledged their disagreement when she was alive or lived up to the moral task of addressing the harm he considered she was doing herself.[50] Has Salim betrayed his mother? And if so, in what way: by not dissuading her from engaging with devils when she was alive; or by violently undoing the relationships she had established with them for herself and for him, after her death, when she could no longer stop him?

Salim's obligations to his mother, as he understands them, conflict with those she had to the spirits. Salim did what he thought best for her, but the decision left a remainder, failing commitments to the spirits that his mother was passing on to him. Salim would affirm that his action was justified. But the devils are offended and persecute him. Put otherwise, Salim feels guilty, and he is punished.[51]

---

50 As Anthony Appiah points out, "In the real world, the act of framing – the act of describing a situation, and thus determining that there's a decision to be made – is itself a moral task. It's often *the* moral task. Learning how to recognize what is and isn't an option is part of our ethical development" (Appiah, *Experiments in Ethics*, 196, as cited by Webb Keane, *Ethical Life*, 249.)

51 Like the protagonists of Greek tragedy, Salim is faced with incompatible, conflicting, or incommensurable claims upon him and has to recognize the authority of both (MacIntyre, *After Virtue*, 134, as cited by Mattingly, *Moral Laboratories*, 108). Yet another way to describe things is to say that Salim suffers guilt by omission. Guilt by omission may play a larger role in human life relative to guilt by commission than we generally give it credit for.

We see both Salim's active *response* to his mother's situation and his passionate *responsivity* as his own situation.[52] But if responsivity is passionate, it is not passive; if Salim seems trapped, that is because he accepts *responsibility*. His response is virtuous insofar as he cares for his mother's well-being. His responsivity is virtuous insofar as he acknowledges failed commitments and feels guilt, explicitly with respect to his mother and implicitly with respect to the spirits. They retaliate, whether because they are offended, to convince him to acknowledge relations, or simply for the malicious pleasure of doing so.

That ethical judgment is not distinct from rational thought is an insight that goes back to Aristotle. As interpreted by Gadamer, phronesis is "concerned with reason and with knowledge, not detached from a being that is becoming, but determined by it and determinative of it."[53] Salim reflects on his condition, rationally, but he also suffers it. He maintains integrity at the expense of well-being. His ethical conflict is embodied, akin to the way Freud saw hysterics frozen in moral dilemma.[54] As Joel Robbins might put it, Salim lives in moral torment.[55]

---

52 On responsivity see Wentzer, "'I Have Seen Königsberg Burning,'" after Waldenfels, *Phenomenology of the Alien*. As Cheryl Mattingly writes, "We simply are not the sort of beings who can be summed up by the categories into which we can be placed or the properties we have, in a third person sort of way. Rather, we have a first person orientation to them, we respond to the categories that 'name' us and the social practices we participate in" (Mattingly, *Moral Laboratories*, 12). One could also say that if Salim interprets the metahumans and Islam, it is equally he who is interpreted.

53 Gadamer, *Truth and Method*, 278, as cited by Bernstein, *Beyond Objectivism*, 38.

54 Breuer and Freud, *Studies on Hysteria*. Like Freud's hysterics, Salim's struggle has a sexual dimension. For a Muslim reformist, sex outside marriage is wrong; for Salim's predecessors and most of his male peers what is strictly forbidden is only penetrative sex with unmarried virgins. The view has been that for available women (*viavy tovu*) sexual relations are a legitimate means of support, and both premarital sex and adultery have been a kind of sport. It is significant that I never heard a Kibushy word for masturbation, suggesting it was not even a salient concept. That Salim holds the reformist position on sex so stringently invites psychoanalytic description. I suspect, but don't know (didn't think to ask ...), that extramarital relations were not a problem for him prior to his mother's death.

55 Robbins, *Becoming Sinners*. As Robert Orsi puts it, "meaning making is wounding" (*Between Heaven and Earth*, 144).

Harry Frankfurt wisely tells us that "What a person really needs to know, in order to know how to live, is what to care about and how to measure the relative importance to him of the various things about which he cares."[56] But this grants too much autonomy to the individual and too much distinctiveness to the alternatives. Salim suffers what Cora Diamond calls a difficulty of reality, "the apparent resistance by reality to one's ordinary mode of life, including one's ordinary modes of thinking: to appreciate the difficulty is to feel oneself being shouldered out of how one thinks, how one is apparently supposed to think, or to have a sense of the inability of thought to encompass what it is attempting to reach. Such appreciation may involve … profound isolation …" Speaking here of Elizabeth Costello, the troubled lecturer of Coetzee's *The Lives of Animals*, Diamond continues: "her isolation is felt in the body…"[57] This describes Salim's situation.

4 The Incommensurability of Concepts

A difficulty of reality suggests that Salim's problem also has to do with his concepts. Before adding another level of description to his case I make some general remarks about our life with concepts.

A number of philosophers have described a distinctive attribute of the human condition as finitude. Our incapacity to resolve our place in the universe, or indeed to conclusively resolve most matters epistemological or ethical, is evident in, and conversely, renders

---

56 Frankfurt, *Taking Ourselves Seriously and Getting It Right*, 28.
57 Diamond, "The Difficulty of Reality and the Difficulty of Philosophy," 12, referring to Coetzee, *The Lives of Animals*. Diamond says, "Coetzee gives us a view of a profound disturbance of soul, and puts that view into a complex context. What is done by doing so he cannot tell us, he does not know. What response we may have to the difficulties of the lectures, the difficulties of reality, is not something the lectures themselves are meant to settle. This itself expresses a mode of understanding of the kind of animal we are, and indeed of the moral life of this kind of animal" ("The Difficulty of Reality," 11). By "lectures" I take it Diamond refers both to Coetzee's Tanner Lectures and to the lectures by Elizabeth Costello as he depicts them.

unsurprising, the diversity of values, concepts, models, and even modes of truth and validation that characterize the human world. One distinctive empirical feature of humanity as a species is that its members endlessly disagree with one another, and sometimes with themselves, not least on what marks distinction. As Lévi-Strauss says in my epigraph, "all problems pertaining *to* humankind are ultimately problems *for* humankind." I take this to be what keeps in motion the conversations that are philosophy and anthropology.[58]

One source of disagreement is located in the nature and application of concepts.[59] The aspect of concepts on which I focus is

58 Lévi-Strauss, "Anthropology and the 'Truth' Sciences," 247. Here is the full quotation: "This is one fundamental weakness – and perhaps also the fundamental greatness – of the humane sciences; that all problems pertaining *to* humankind are ultimately problems *for* humankind. There is no problem, however small, that does not concern each of us, because our life interests, our personal history, our temperament, our prejudices are immediately implicated in every problem. This is probably the reason why the social sciences should not pretend to reach truth, which is probably impossible of attainment, but more modestly some amount of wisdom – the achievement of which is supremely difficult, as a matter of fact. But if we are able to make even some limited progress towards wisdom, then we may be – and this is perhaps our advantage – we may be more ready to resign ourselves to the general truth that science will remain forever incomplete" (emphasis in original). Natural science aside, I suggest this means we cannot conceive of our address of human problems in terms of an external measure of progress. This lecture is merely one turn in a long conversation.

59 Obviously, there are other sources of human disagreement, including interest, habit, conviction, and prior investment or commitment. I take concepts as abstract objects of thought that mediate and organize experience. Concepts are of course central to both philosophy and cognitive science, and it is not my intention to weigh in on the extensive debates about them. On the philosophical view generally, see Margolis and Laurence, "Concepts," and for one that informs this lecture, Diamond, "Losing Your Concepts." To attempt to define "concept" more precisely would be to go against the very concept of the concept developed here. An anthropological view, in which "concepts" displace the older language of "symbols," and possibly the Peircean architecture of "signs," is not yet well articulated, but Das offers a significant opening, drawing from Wittgenstein and Diamond to suggest that concepts grow out of life and as we live with them, and do not, in the general run of things, have fixed

that, like values, they are often incommensurable with one other, that is, *without an external common measure between them.* This does *not* imply that such concepts are either logically incompatible or incomparable, but it does indicate that there is no single or objectively correct way to relate them with one another.[60] This means that we are likely both to continue to debate them and to talk past each other.[61]

It is evident that concepts and their authority change over time, what Ian Hacking has called historical ontology.[62] An exemplary illustration is Lorraine Daston's account of three successive yet historically overlapping concepts of "nature" in Western thought (as

---

boundaries. "A discussion of ethical life would entail, then, not only what words like good or bad mean but also what *we* – the ones who use them – mean by these words and how we show that they matter" (Das, "What Does Ordinary Ethics Look Like?" 62). To follow a point made by Cavell, we learn our criteria through our judgments (though surely our judgments are also based on criteria, even if tacit ones).

60 On incommensurability I draw from Kuhn, *The Structure of Scientific Revolutions*; Rorty, *Philosophy and the Mirror of Nature*; and especially Bernstein, *Beyond Objectivism*. For Rorty, incommensurable ideas or discourses are those not "able to be brought under a set of rules which will tell us how rational agreement can be reached ... where statements seem to conflict" (Rorty, *Philosophy and the Mirror of Nature*, 316; see also Bernstein, *Beyond Objectivism*, 85–6). Incommensurability also means, as Jacqueline Solway has reminded me, that ideas are not reducible to each other or to something they have in common. How we can distinguish whether alien beliefs are incommensurable with ours, or either similar, inconsistent, or incompatible, is a central question for anthropology, albeit rarely recognized as such. Some help is offered in Diamond "Criticising from 'Outside,'" and implicitly in Gadamer, *Truth and Method*.

61 As Nietzsche put it, "Every concept arises from the equation of unequal things" (Nietzsche, "On Truth and Lying in an Extra-Moral Sense," 17). The citation is taken from Ann Laura Stoler, *Duress: Imperial Durabilities in Our Times*, 14. Operating in a very different context from mine, Stoler is likewise concerned that anthropologists pay closer attention to the life of concepts. She notes that concepts are embedded in "relations of force" and that "the fictions of their 'stability'... entail violences of their own" (17); hence that we "look to the unmarked space between their porous and policed peripheries" (9).

62 Hacking, *Historical Ontology*. See also his *Social Construction of What?*

specific, local, and universal), each with different implications for how it might serve to legitimate or simply illustrate conceptions of morality.[63] Although Daston does not use the term, these concepts of nature are incommensurable with one another, suggesting that no one of them is sufficient – that is, able to consistently and comprehensively correspond to a world or truth independent of it or to everything we would want to say about it. This is not to say that any of them are wrong or that an incompatible concept would serve us better.[64] It is not to adopt an idealist or extreme relativist position, but it is to suggest that there is a fundamental gap between human concepts and their ostensible referents, between human language and thought, on the one side, and the non- or extra-human world on the other.[65] The human recognition of this distinction, in its various manifestations, is what anthropologists call the nature/culture problem. This is complex insofar as "nature" and "culture" are themselves concepts (and contested ones), hence each in the realm of "culture," yet also ostensibly the objects to which they refer, hence each a part of "nature" in a broad sense. In effect, this indexes exactly the nature/culture problem; it *is* that problem.[66]

---

63 Daston, "The Morality of Natural Orders." "The first, venerable conception of nature is literally specific: that which makes something the kind (or species) of thing it is, its ontological identity card, if you will ... This specific sense of nature is closely related to a second kind of natural order conceived as local, pertaining to the flora, fauna, and landscape of a particular place. Both specific and local natural orders are richly variable, cornucopias of types and topographies. They are regular, but not deterministic, orders based on 'what happens always or most of the time,' in Aristotle's phrase, rather than on inexorable physical necessity. The third, more modern conception of nature is by contrast comprehensive, uniform, and universal. It embraces the entire nonhuman universe and is designed by unexceptionable regularities that are everywhere and always the same" (375). Compare Raymond Williams, *Keywords*, on "nature" (184–9) and on the history, and what he calls the "difficulty," of certain words more generally.

64 Note that these are concepts, not competing theories or testable hypotheses.

65 The position is well described in Bernstein's title, after Gadamer, as "beyond objectivism and relativism."

66 Ryle, *The Concept of Mind*, would say they are of different logical types.

In speaking of incommensurability between language or concepts and world I am not suggesting incompatibility. But if there is a fundamental incommensurability *between* thought and world, conceptions of the world are likely to be disparate, leaving room for other conceptions that do not simply oppose or negate each other as offer incommensurate, non-exclusive alternatives *to each other* with respect to the world.[67] Many of our intellectual differences are of this order. This is a different matter from whether any given concepts provide true or false or more or less accurate or effective pictures.[68]

Sometimes we mistake incommensurable concepts for commensurable ones. These fall into pairs, like body and mind, that are often taken as what I consider false binary oppositions, false in the sense that they do not have a common external measure or facet by which they can be discriminated from one another and hence are strictly neither binary nor opposed.[69] Mistaking incommensurability for commensurability in this way could be a category mistake, in Ryle's sense of allocating "concepts to logical types to which they do not belong."[70]

---

67 To clarify, one could call the incommensurability between concepts and world primary or vertical, and the incommensurability of concepts with one another secondary or horizontal. Wittgenstein draws sparingly on the concept of the incommensurable (*inkommensurabel*), but when he does so, it is in the first sense, with respect to the relationship between concepts and experiences. As Juliet Floyd puts it (personal communication, 17 June 2018), "It may remain unclear what is meant by a 'concept,' but still, whatever it is, a concept is supposed to be something *general*, made to apply to possibly more than one thing (even if it happens that as a matter of fact there is only one thing). The whole difficulty is that experiences are *singular*, but we are constantly sorting them *via* concepts." Relevant passages in Wittgenstein are Item 162b (a pocket notebook from 1939–40) 27rff, "Words and experience incommensurable" and Manuscript 120, 90rff, "Is not the 'inner' process of focusing on the pain incommensurable with the expression of the thought?" I am indebted to Juliet Floyd for these references.

68 I leave these tough questions to philosophers.

69 I take "binary" in the Saussurean sense of the presence of a distinctive feature, as is the case with neighbouring phonemes.

70 Ryle, *The Concept of Mind*, 17.

Other concepts are notable for their singularity or self-sufficiency. Take *sila*, a Greenlandic concept comprehending weather but also "the air; the outside; the world; a person's mind, consciousness, and senses."[71] The concept of the human, which she is at pains to distinguish from "member of a species," is singular for Cora Diamond.[72] "The human" here does not exist in any simple binary opposition, whether to the animal, the inhuman, nonhuman, superhuman, etc. Whereas there is something deeply evident about this for Diamond, Eduardo Viveiros de Castro suggests that interesting concepts say "something nonevident about the world," as *sila* certainly does for "us."[73]

The incommensurability of concepts is most evident when we find them untranslatable between languages (and perhaps undefinable in their own language), as the incomparable *Dictionary of Untranslatables* makes evident.[74] *Geist*, for example, is simply not the equivalent of "mind." As speech communities learn new words for which they have no equivalent they accumulate incommensurable concepts drawn from different sources. Scientific or religious paradigms may decisively succeed each other, but more common is what Daston shows and what German historiographers have called "the contemporaneity of the non-contemporaneous," as older concepts perdure alongside newer ones.[75] Take the English words "ethics" and "morality," drawn respectively from Greek

---

71 Nuttall, "Arctic Weather Words." See also Nuttall, *Arctic Homeland*.
72 Diamond, "Losing Your Concepts," esp. 265.
73 Viveiros de Castro, "The Relative Native," 496.
74 As Barbara Cassin says, "to speak of untranslatables in no way implies that the terms in question ... are not and cannot be translated: the untranslatable is rather what one keeps on (not) translating" (*Dictionary of Untranslatables*, xvii). The *Dictionary* restricts itself to European languages; a more global or anthropological one remains to be compiled. Certain untranslatables function as what Sherry Ortner called key symbols ("On Key Symbols"), untranslatable because of all they condense. I suspect that concepts commensurable with one another within a given language more readily find their equivalents in other languages than do concepts that are incommensurable with others within a single language.
75 Koselleck, *Futures Past*; the phrase in German is the *Gleichzeitigkeit der Ungleichzeitigen*.

and Latin. Outside the explicit models of individual philosophers, they do not fit commensurably with one another, and when we try to commensurate such models with those of other philosophers, we get greater confusion. Or perhaps "confusion" is the wrong description, and we just have a more realistic picture of life with concepts. Messiness is sometimes less distorting than clarity. Even someone who can distinguish concepts with such precision as Austin remarks that "We may cheerfully use ... terms which are not so much head-on incompatible as simply disparate, which just do not fit in or even on."[76] This has been the case for a number of the concepts of metahumans prevalent in Mayotte and perhaps for metahumans more generally.

Faced with the incommensurable concepts that constitute our forms of life, we exercise practical judgment as we draw on them, whether within a given language game or in distinguishing between games (which themselves may be incommensurable with one another). Discerning among concepts is practical in much the way that Aristotle describes ethical judgment. Indeed, if ethical and aesthetical judgments are not distinguishable from each other on logical grounds, the same could be said of intellectual judgments (with the possible exceptions of framed activities like pure logic and mathematics).[77].

In his famous discussion of "essentially contested concepts," W.B. Gallie noted that an "argument put forward by one side in an apparently endless dispute can be recognized to have a definite

---

76 The passage continues, "Just as we cheerfully subscribe to, or have the grace to be torn between, simply disparate ideals – why *must* there be a conceivable amalgam, the Good Life for Man?" Austin, "A Plea for Excuses," 203, n1.

77 The foundation of mathematics itself remains subject to debate among Platonists (realists), logicists, intuitionists, and formalists; adherence to one or the other position rests on judgment not proof. See Joachim Lambek, "Foundations of Mathematics," accessed 30 March 2018, https://www .britannica.com/science/foundations-of-mathematics/, and for a position they call constructive nominalism, Joachim Lambek and Philip Scott, "Reflections on the Categorical Foundations of Mathematics."

logical force by the other."[78] Hence logic by itself will not resolve the matter, and the differences cannot be put down to irrationality. Gallie describes the situation as one in which, "it is quite impossible to find a general principle for deciding which of two contestant uses of an essentially contested concept really 'uses it best.'"[79]

I take essential contestability to be a function of incommensurability. Thus, the concept of "art" is contestable because its relations to neighbouring concepts like craft and skill, science and literature, beauty and value are not self-evident.[80] Gallie proposes that to understand such concepts is, in a sense, to compare them with themselves – that is, compare different uses of the concept rather than attempting to commensurate them with each other or with neighbouring concepts.[81] However, Gallie concludes that the "exigencies of living" mean it may be impossible to remain uncommitted to every one of the contested alternatives.[82]

---

78 Gallie, "Essentially Contested Concepts," 190.
79 Gallie, "Essentially Contested Concepts," 189.
80 Gallie also mentions democracy, religion, and social justice as essentially contested concepts. Geertz applies it to "ethnographic assertion" ("Thick Description," 29), not itself a concept in the same way. I would add to Gallie's list culture, nature, and mind.
81 "Commonly we come to see more precisely what a given scientific concept means by contrasting its deductive powers with those of other closely related concepts: in the case of an appraisive concept, we can best see more precisely what it means by comparing and contrasting our uses of it now with other earlier uses of it or its progenitors, i.e., by considering how it came to be" (Gallie, "Essentially Contested Concepts," 198). Gallie does not cite another philosopher, though I take it his position may be influenced by Wittgenstein and suggests Nietzsche's (and subsequently Foucault's) concept of genealogy.
82 Gallie, "Essentially Contested Concepts," 190. Gallie argues that "Reason, according to so many great philosophical voices, is essentially something which demands and deserves universal assent – the manifestation of whatever makes for unity among men and/or the constant quest for such beliefs as could theoretically be accepted as satisfactory by all men. This account of reason may be adequate so long as our chief concern is with the use or manifestation of reason in science; but it fails completely as a description of those elements of reason that make possible discussions of religious, political and artistic problems." But he adds, "Since the Enlightenment a number of brilliant thinkers seem positively to have

Diamond develops the implications. "In our cognitive activities we may be aiming at getting things right, but how we carry on these activities, how we understand what 'getting it right' might involve or might cost in the particular case, reveals our own nature as moral beings."[83] It follows, Diamond says, that "If *thought* is seen as inherently or ubiquitously moral, then we need to reject the idea that moral thought is a *department* of thought, and moral discourse a *department* of discourse."[84]

This is why I find the phrase "anthropology of ethics" a misleading conceptualization of the intellectual project in which I have been engaged.[85] Said otherwise, the ethical is one kind of description under which to place human thought and action, one kind of description under which people can put their circumstances, concerns, dilemmas, and attachments to the world and to other persons. It is not a discrete department of thought or action.

When incommensurable values or concepts are subject to practical reason in context, what seems the better alternative is followed,

---

exulted in emphasising the irrational elements in our thinking in these latter fields. My purpose in this paper has been to combat, and in some measure correct, this dangerous tendency." All page 196.

83 Diamond, "'We Are Perpetually Moralists,'" 103. While I might replace the term "nature" with "condition," I agree with the general point. The relation of the practical, the moral, and understanding is also a theme of Gadamer, for whom "understanding itself is a form of practical reasoning" (Bernstein, *Beyond Objectivism*, 174).

84 Diamond, "'We Are Perpetually Moralists,'" 104. Bernard Williams makes compatible observations in *Shame and Necessity*, arguing against the idea that our moral sense is characterless or that we can operate by means of pure reason.

85 If the ethical or moral is not a "department" of thought or discourse, so its study should not be a "department" of anthropology. Whether the case be different for philosophy is not for me to say. Elizabeth Anderson perceptively transcends such departmental distinctions in her discussion in *Value in Ethics and Economics* and offers somewhat parallel thought with respect to reasoning, describing her approach as "a 'rational attitude theory,' according to which the attitudes engaged when we care about things involve not just feelings but judgment, conduct, sensitivities to qualities in what we value, and certain ways of structuring deliberation concerned with what we value" (5).

but at the "cost" or with a "remainder" of what the alternatives have to offer.[86] Such is the situation in which Salim finds himself.

5 Salim's Conceptual Difficulty

Salim's difficulty stems from his life with concepts as much as his life with persons. Despite being best friends with his mother, Salim had come to place her actions under descriptions different from hers.[87]

For his mother and for Vita there is a conceptual distinction between immoral, diffuse, and relatively impersonal *sheitwan*, who tempt us into misdeeds, and amoral beings called *djinn, lulu,* or sometimes also *sheitwan*, with whom one can establish positive personal relations. This is less a difference between discrete kinds of metapersons than a case of incommensurable concepts of metabeings and incommensurable language games. Salim attempts to fit them all under one concept and game as *sheitwan*, generic beings who bring only harm and ultimately damnation.[88] Hence,

---

86 On remainders, see Foot, "Moral Realism and Moral Dilemma," and Bernard Williams, "Ethical Consistency" and "Consistency and Realism." There is undoubtedly much more to say here.

87 They may have shared concepts of divine expectation and of punishment in the afterlife, but these became much sharper and more immediate for Salim. And of course, Salim has an additional concept that his mother lacked, namely bullshit.

88 In Mayotte there are several concepts of metapersons. Some metahumans belong to named classes, and the members of some of these are individuated as distinct persons. But insofar as metahumans are amorphous, multiple, and generally not visible, and insofar as the concepts and terms are drawn from several traditions and languages, the distinctions among them are not always clear. One could say the terms have no external referent or object for which they stand but find their meaning only through use in specific language games. They are subject to misunderstanding from those who are not fully playing or who don't wish to or cannot follow the same rules as the chief players. And they are taken up in new language games that may be incommensurable with their uses in other games. We easily reach the situation described by Ryle (*Dilemmas*) where players of adjacent games can only misunderstand

whereas I once explicitly rejected the translation of *djinn* as "*diables*" for "spirits" in English,[89] Salim used the English word "devils" indiscriminately.

In effect, he takes two concepts of metapersons that people accommodate in coexistence insofar as they are incommensurable with one another, redescribes them as incompatible, and rejects

---

each other. Salim draws on a salient concept of *sheitwan* as amorphous beings who induce humans to temptation, in a language game that speaks to human inclinations to do wrong. When excusing bad behaviour, or describing lack of self-control, one might attribute it to *sheitwan*. But the word *sheitwan* can also be used as a synonym for *djinn* to refer to distinct kinds of beings, similar to humans, but of different substance and with different powers. *Djinn* can be classified and individuated and can develop intimate relations with people and speak through ("possess") them. In the case of Salim's mother these were *patros*; these are *djinn* bearing names from Arabic manuscripts but said to be indigenous to Mayotte. Their appearance is similar to *trumba*, manifestations of deceased Malagasy rulers, hence not strictly *djinn* at all, but classifiable under the generic Malagasy term *lulu*, which is often used for *djinn* and other kinds of metahumans as well. See Lambek, *Human Spirits,* for fuller description and argument.

89 "*Diables*" was the term found in earlier French sources, and it is possible that Salim uses "devils" because he is translating from Kibushy via French, though the term "*esprits*" is also used. "Spirits" brings its own semantic baggage but is ethically neutral. I have written a good deal about what is called spirit possession, arguing that initiation to mediumship in Mayotte entails socializing the individual amoral spirit. It never becomes fully social or moral – a tension always remains, and this is part of what makes things so compelling – but once you establish terms, it will look out for you and your family (Lambek, *Human Spirits*). People's relations with metapersons are significant not only, or even primarily, in moments of active "possession" (trance) but in living alongside them. That is to say, mediums become temporarily and periodically "actively" possessed by metapersons with whom they cohabit continuously and over the long term, and whose presence manifests in such things as the maintenance of restrictions (*fady*, taboos). Moreover, such metapersons can develop personal relationships with others in the medium's circle, notably with members of her family, as the metahumans living with Salim's mother tried to do with him. To make a broad analogy, a musician has a relationship with her instrument and her musicianship even at moments when she is not actively playing, as do close others, even when they are not listening to her play.

one. He is able to conceive metahumans only as *sheitwan*. His concepts are impoverished.

From the perspective of his mother or Vita, this could be understood as part of a broader mistake.[90] Whereas Vita lives a life in which being a pious Muslim and an adept of spirits are evident alongside one another, for Salim they are mutually exclusive.

I'd like to describe this as the outcome of a category mistake.[91] As such, it is not Salim's alone but that of a whole movement of reformist Islam.[92] In drawing such a boundary, in attempting to live in this manner, Salim joins large numbers of people across the globe, not only Muslims, and including many scientists, who see the world in terms of incompatible concepts and mutually exclusive alternatives.[93] To the degree that such movements are successful, there is no longer a category error but a new description of the world. However, in this instance, as in many others, the shift remains contested and incomplete, and Salim is caught on the crux. *Both descriptions hold.* The metahumans are demonic *sheitwan* as a result of his reconceptualization of their nature, yet they are also

---

90 Anthropologists used to deny that our informants make mistakes. If we call their ideas irrational it is only because we do not understand them. But just as we readily make mistakes within our own thought, so do other people. Moreover, the mistakes at issue are manifestations not of irrationality but of Wittgensteinian "non-sense" or grammar. Additionally, I describe Salim's move as a mistake not from the perspective of a full outsider but from that of an insider, like Vita or Salim's mother, for whom certain metahumans are complex interesting beings with whom it is possible to establish mutually beneficial relations so long as you stand up for yourself and treat each other with respect.

91 It is equivalent to short-circuiting the mind-body problem by adopting a pure physicalist position.

92 Islamic reform here manifests as what Webb Keane in *Ethical Life*, after Bernard Williams, *Ethics and the Limits of Philosophy*, might call a morality system and what Jack Sidnell, "Ethical Projects, or How to Bring about a Way of Life" (unpublished paper) rephrases as an ethical project. Salim is striving to become a better person and is frustrated that he cannot live up to his ideals. On the ethical dimension of Muslim piety, see Mahmood, *The Politics of Piety*.

93 We surely all confront what we understand as mutually exclusive alternatives at times, and sometimes they are truly inconsistent with one another such that a definitive choice is necessary.

human-like *djinn,* open to establishing positive relations. Salim is not able to maintain an absolute distinction; in practice the concepts remain incommensurable, even though he claims otherwise.

Category mistakes and their consequences take place in historical time, not in the abstract. The situation is one of the contemporaneity of the non-contemporaneous. Salim lives in a world in which piety and cohabitation with *djinn* are *both* compatible with one another, if incommensurable, *and* incompatible, conflicting, and mutually exclusive.[94] Salim asserts the second model. But on personal and practical grounds he cannot fully reject the first model, both because of his relations with his mother and because the metahumans themselves will not release him. Salim is stuck between affirming that he will not live *with* these metahumans and suspecting he cannot live *without* them.[95]

It is evident that Salim is entangled with metahumans in their aspects both as persons and as concepts. Conceptually, his mistake is what Wittgenstein might call non-sense, a mistake in grammar rather than in reasoning, albeit non-sense that becomes the basis for sense in a new language game.[96] Personally, his mistake lies in violating commitments, with the repercussions he reports.

---

94 Bernstein, *Beyond Objectivism,* clarifies the distinction between incompatibility and incommensurability. Statements or theories are incompatible if they entail a logical contradiction. This presupposes a common logical framework. With incommensurability there is no neutral framework or language along which the two rival paradigms can be fully expressed (85). In *Knowledge and Practice in Mayotte,* I argued that three incommensurable traditions of knowledge – Islam, astrology, and spirit possession – coexisted with one another in practice in Mayotte. I found something roughly equivalent in subsequent research in Switzerland with respect to the coexistence, conversation, and practical cross-overs among biomedicine, Christianity, and various alternative and esoteric traditions of complementary medicine, anthroposophy, and the like.

95 If this argument appears convoluted, I can only say that it corresponds to the situation in which Salim finds himself. Note that I am *not* suggesting a direct cause-and-effect relationship between the mistake and Salim's condition.

96 For informed arguments concerning what Wittgenstein intends by nonsense and the implications for religion and theology, see Mulhall, *The Great Riddle.*

Salim's mistakes are not an inevitable outcome of a shift to reformist Islam. Zara, a woman whose initial possession ceremonies I attended and who subsequently treated spirits in newer adepts, wanted to withdraw from possession activities as she became more pious. She asked the spirits to leave her and began a regime of prayer to encourage them to do so. In this manner she was able gracefully to extricate herself from relations with them and to do so without any conceptual confusion.[97]

6 Both/And

Here is my description of the situation at its most abstract. Mayotte has been a world in which people live *both* as good Muslims *and* cohabiting with spirits. An alternative paradigm suggests one can live *either* as a good Muslim *or* trafficking in spirits, but not both. The pluralist "and" world is challenged by the exclusionary "either/or" one.[98] Salim is caught between them: his situation is at once either/or *and* both/and.

Salim's difficulties are shaped by the historical context. A similar kind of structural tension, albeit not necessarily experienced as painful, is characteristic of life with any strong pair of incommensurable concepts, such as mind/body or nature/culture, that appear as false binary oppositions. We both conceptualize them as mutually exclusive domains *and* we live with them as two aspects of a single whole. If plurality of values entails contestability, so life with concepts entails inconsistency.

---

97 Eventually Zara could hear the music of a possession ceremony with equanimity, without feeling pulled in; as she told me, this indicated that the *djinn* had fully left her. Zara's situation is of course different from Salim's in a number of respects that I cannot address here. Among other things, Zara was never reputed to engage in sorcery.

98 These alternatives are of course ideal types. Either/or oppositions occur at multiple loci and levels of scale and recursion. I do not take them to be either fully encompassing or fully determining.

One question then is how we respond to inconsistency, acknowledging, ignoring, or denying it.[99] Acknowledging inconsistency can manifest as irony. In ways that both Alexander Nehamas and Jonathan Lear have shown, irony can be serious and sincere in holding finality in suspension.[100] Irony can also be realistic; as Stephen Mulhall says with respect to literature, "aspiring to a genuine mimesis of reality very often requires the establishment of an ironic relation to it."[101]

Now, irony happens to be a trait I once argued is intrinsic to the multiple voicing characteristic of possession by spirits, of never being quite certain who is speaking when.[102] Public performances highlight this ironic mode of being. For example, those spirits (*trumba*) who manifest former monarchs who were Muslim in life remain so in their post-mortem appearances, despite the fact that

---

99 Inconsistency is characteristic not only of the application of false binaries but with respect to living with any set of concepts and practices drawn from incommensurable traditions.

100 Nehamas, *The Art of Living*, draws from Socratic and Platonic irony, whereas Lear, *Therapeutic Action* and *A Case for Irony*, attends more to Kierkegaard and Freud. Irony, says Lear, is "a manifestation of a practical understanding of one aspect of the finiteness of human life: that the concepts with which we understand ourselves and live our lives have a certain vulnerability built into them. Ironic existence thus has a claim to be a human excellence because it is a form of truthfulness. It is also a form of self-knowledge: A practical acknowledgment of the kind of knowing that is available to creatures like us" (excerpt from *A Case for Irony*, http://www.hup.harvard.edu/features/irony-and-humanity/). This raises the question what kind of truth it is to deny inconsistency – to take conceptual distinctions literally.

101 Mulhall, *The Great Riddle*.

102 To be more specific, there is uncertainty regarding who is animator, author, and principal, in Goffman's sense of footing. See Goffman, "Footing." And especially where multiple spirits are present, there is also dramatic irony, as elucidated by Burke, *A Grammar of Motives*, or Bakhtin, *The Dialogic Imagination* – that is, where each character necessarily offers a perspective on the standpoints of each of the others and hence in which no single voice can be understood as strictly true or false but rather contributory to the whole. On personal irony in spirit possession, see Lambek, "Rheumatic Irony." See also Boddy, *Wombs and Alien Spirits*.

Islam denies in principle their very existence. Moreover, those who were poor Muslims during life, remain so after death, revealing in their performances that they are hiding bottles of liquor in their robes ...[103] All this speaks to a joyous and playful recognition of life lived as both/and that subsumes either/or – both Islam *and* cohabiting with spirits, both prohibition *and* alcohol.

Irony is not always easy; sometimes it is impossible to see both the rabbit and the duck at once or difficult to keep both in mind. However, once acknowledged, irony need not preclude principled judgment; indeed, a sense for irony may be critical for moral wisdom, for cross-cultural understanding, and for insight in a psychoanalytic sense.[104]

As for anthropologists, we need another look at inconsistency. Lévi-Strauss revolutionized anthropological thinking about ordinary ("undomesticated") thought, demonstrating how it manifests as the play of classificatory schemes along multiple axes of difference. However, as Diamond argues, classification is insufficient to describe how we live with concepts. She perceives an "underlying inadequacy in a philosophical view of language that ties description to classification." She writes that, "grasping a concept (even one like that of a human being, which is a descriptive concept if any are) is not a matter just of knowing how to group things under that concept; it is being able to participate in life-with-the-concept."[105]

---

103 Lambek, *Knowledge and Practice in Mayotte*; Lambek, *The Weight of the Past*.

104 To return to Salim, would a solution to his impasse come through conceptual clarification, reordering personal relations with the *djinn*, addressing unconscious issues with his mother, acknowledging the irony of his situation, or from some combination? Is this what a local cure might accomplish? Is it his mother's situation that needs to be put under a new description or Salim's own, and is it possible to accomplish both? What form of ethically satisfactory cohabitation is possible? Insofar as spirit possession is redescribed, and hence reconceived, as a kind of living alongside oneself, this is what Salim appears unable (or unwilling) to do.

105 Both passages are from Diamond, "Losing Your Concepts," 266. The latter continues: "What kinds of descriptive concept there are is a matter of the different shapes life-with-a-concept can have. Life with the concept human being is very different from life with the concept member of the

She suggests that we "get rid of the idea that using a concept is a matter of using it to pick out what falls under the concept and what does not … [and] see instead that life with a concept involves doings and thinkings and understandings of many sorts, into which one's grasp of the concept enters in different ways."[106]

Putting things under description is thus not intrinsically the same as putting them into mutually exclusive classes.

This is necessarily the case when we address Gallie's "essentially contested" concepts or those I have described as incommensurable with one another. Nevertheless, one of the things we humans do with concepts *is* to attempt to classify and oppose them and hence to make category mistakes.[107] Living with concepts includes making and living with these mistakes.

---

species Homo sapiens. To be able to use the concept 'human being' is to be able to think about human life and what happens in it; it is not to be able to pick human beings out from other things or recommend that certain things be done to them or by them. The criticism I am making could be put this way: linguistic philosophers have brought to their study of language an impoverished view of what can be involved in conceptual life" (266).

106 Diamond, "Losing Your Concepts," 276. This complicates my initial discussion of putting acts under description, given the need to recognize that such descriptions are contingent rather than definitive.

107 Perhaps the broader error could be described as confusing reference and sense. I do not know whether Ryle would find my use of category mistakes too broad or whether Diamond would approve my adding category mistakes to her argument. Ryle offers a broader picture in his Tarner Lectures: "Some thinkers are at loggerheads with one another, not because their propositions do conflict, but because their authors fancy that they conflict. They suppose themselves to be giving, at least by indirect implication, rival answers to the same questions, when this is not really the case. They are then talking at cross-purposes with one another. It can be convenient to characterize these cross-purposes by saying that the two sides are, at certain points, hinging their arguments upon concepts of different categories, though they suppose themselves to be hinging them upon different concepts of the same category, or vice versa. But it is not more than convenient. It still remains to be shown that the discrepancies are discrepancies of this general kind, and this can be done only by showing in detail how the métiers in ratiocination of the concepts under pressure are more dissimilar from one another or

The fact that we recognize a category mistake does not mean that we can overcome it or that in overcoming it we do not replace it with another category mistake. If for Ryle category mistakes are errors of logical typing, it is a feature of life with certain concepts that we are not always able intellectually to keep differences of logical type fully in our sights or interested practically in doing so.[108] It may even be that certain realms of thought or structures of practice must rest on category mistakes.[109]

Finally, I am sceptical whether there is a neutral, Archimedean place from which to discern what is a category mistake; this illustrates again the inseparability of reason and judgment. In describing Salim's position as mistaken, I have revealed my partiality. Writing from an appreciation of irony and life with spirits, I regret the turn Salim has taken. In a way, this lecture is addressed to him. But if

---

less dissimilar from one another than the contestants had unwittingly supposed" (*Dilemmas*, 11). To the best of my knowledge, Diamond does not cite Ryle. An example of a category mistake with which we live is a division of academic disciplines into "arts" and "sciences" (and as if it were obvious into which category linguistics, mathematics, or anthropology fit) whereas recognizing the incommensurability of these concepts leads to more interesting conversations.

108 Living with concepts as Diamond describes it is different from making category mistakes but not necessarily incompatible. Diamond's view of life with a concept is undoubtedly closer to Salim's experience, while category mistakes can only be seen from a distance. It may take an anthropologist or philosopher to force us to recognize that our ordinary and often quite contented and creative life with concepts is one that draws on category mistakes.

109 Here are two sources of conceptual mistakes: (a) mistaking incommensurable concepts for commensurable or incompatible ones; and (b) mistaking equally valid descriptions of the same phenomenon, taken from different angles or at different levels of proximity, as either mutually exclusive or as describing two quite different phenomena. There is also the common mistaking of the metaphorical for the literal and vice versa. I committed the latter when I wrote about a sea monster in Mayotte responsible for several drownings, only to discover on a subsequent visit that people had been referring to an electric sting ray that had been lurking in the shallows, with power enough to stun children who would fall and drown (*Island in the Stream*). In effect, I had substituted a concept of my own imagination.

he misses the point, or simply lives differently with his concepts, or lives with different concepts, he does so from his own stance, here perhaps less as a European intellectual who reads Voltaire than as a pious Muslim concerned with the afterlife, but after all, both.

7 Metapersons

Once we think of concepts as not only tools for thought but singular and dynamic companions, it is evident that, as with persons, we need to acknowledge our vulnerability to them and their vulnerability to us.[110] Living with diverse concepts, like living with persons, entails multiple and sometimes competing commitments and obligations, and the continuous exercise of judgment in responding to each. Both concepts and persons can be more or less reliable or contestable. With both persons and concepts, we take into consideration their relations with one another as well as directly with us. We try to stabilize and order our concepts by means of definitions, classification, arguments, or theoretical frameworks, and we try to ensure our relations with persons by means of performatively declared and enacted commitments. Yet, acknowledging a person differs from knowing a concept, and believing *in* a person is different from drawing *on* a concept. We may debate *about* a concept but *with* persons. With persons, our emotional and contractual investments are more explicit; we establish expectations that are met with response or silence. Concepts don't get jealous or retaliate. You cannot be rewarded or punished, loved or rejected, pursued or ignored, condemned or forgiven by a concept as you can by a person.

Except when the concepts are realized as metapersons.

The metapersons in question are gods, demons, saints, and spirits, who can make powerful interventions in human lives.[111] Insofar

---

110 To be clear, I am not equating or commensurating persons and concepts; each exceeds the other in interesting ways.

111 One could compare the characters of literature or history or public figures. As people in Mayotte are condemned or privileged to live with *djinn*, so

as they belong at once to realms of thought and sociality, I suggest that they are simultaneously both concepts and persons.[112] Meta-humans overlap with Lévi-Strauss's concrete signifiers insofar as they are imagined with respect to their appearance and properties in relation to other characters with contrasting properties. But as concepts they are not simply signs, and as persons they can act as relatively autonomous, unpredictable beings, valued for their singularity. Like the Greek gods, they can each condense a range of functions, conceived more or less abstractly.[113] In other words,

---

we are all privileged to live with exemplars like Gandhi and Mandela, Diamond, Coetzee, and Elizabeth Costello, and condemned to cohabit with dangerous caricatures like Putin and Trump. North Americans live with metapersons (or para-persons) of many kinds – from the Christian Trinity, through celebrities, literary characters and figures (Helen Mirren, Jane Tennison, *and* "the hard-boiled detective"), comic super-heroes, extraterrestrials, or the voice on our cellphones. On moral exemplars see Humphrey, "Exemplars and Rules." Our relations and commitments are of course different in the case of faith in a deity, persecution by a demon, investment in a theorist, identification with a literary character, adulation of a celebrity, or repulsion by a politician. But insofar as they can each be considered metapersons rather than simply persons, they operate in our lives in ways comparable to concepts and in some instances *as* concepts, or vehicles for concepts, as Freud signifies psychoanalysis, Hitler evil, and so on. Conversely, persons and metapersons can be abstracted, as Hermes lent himself to hermeneutics or Marx to Marxism. We move easily between Kant, Kantianism, and categorical imperative or between structure, structuralism, and Lévi-Strauss. Compare Gilles Deleuze and Félix Guattari's account of "conceptual personae" in *What Is Philosophy?*, chapter 3. From a very different locus, Veena Das recounts how ninth- and tenth-century Sanskrit grammarians thought of words as lonely and seeking company in sentences ("Resemblance and Resonance.")

112 It would be more heavy-handed than I want to describe metahumans as the anthropomorphization of concepts or the abstraction of persons, but these are not entirely false pictures either.

113 On the Greeks, as analysed by classicists influenced by structuralism, see Detienne, *Comparative Anthropology of Ancient Greece,* as well as work with or by Jean-Pierre Vernant and Pierre Vidal-Naquet; also Parker, *On Greek Religion.* My thanks to Barbara Kowalzig for discussion. Hindu or Yoruba deities, Catholic saints, and Malagasy *trumba* are each internally distinguished along different lines. But generally, in polytheistic worlds, concepts, features, and functions are distributed in partial structures

people *think* with them. Cohabitation also entails social relations, characterized by power and intimacy, trust and expectation. Humans find themselves soliciting, repulsing, serving, or deferring to metahumans – and unsure of their responses.[114] In contrast to reified abstractions, metapersons point firmly to the lived and actual aspects of concepts rather than to an essential nature or misplaced concreteness.[115] Whereas to reify is to opt for static, bounded entities, to personify is to mark uncertainty, ambivalence, and possible disappointment, but also to anticipate surprise, natality, trust, and grace.[116]

Whether metahumans are better understood as concepts or as persons are concerns implicit to practical religion and explicit to theology.[117] With respect to ordinary practice, distinguishing cohab-

---

    or family resemblances among figures who each attract diverse human commitments.

114 See Orsi, *Between Heaven and Earth,* for a compelling account of intimate relations with Catholic saints; Sahlins, "The Original Political Society," for a comparative review of relations with metahumans conceived politically. Metahumans can be dominant; in describing the entry of a spirit to one's head, my mentor Tumbu seized my arm hard and, switching from Kibushy to French, exclaimed "*coup d'état!*" They can be predatory, as Salim experienced; provoke fear and awe, as Otto, *The Idea of the Holy,* describes; elicit deference, as portrayed in Bloch, "Ritual and Deference"; or remain elusive and disinterested. Encounters can also be exhilarating and joyous. (I do not think there is an essentially religious experience.)

115 See Whitehead, *Science and the Modern World,* on misplaced concreteness, and James, *The Meaning of Truth,* on what he called vicious abstractions. See also Kenny, "Anthropomorphism vs Humanism," for the comparable concept of "vicious anthropomorphisms." One of the virtues of structuralism is its ability to avoid premature objectification.

116 "The fact that man is capable of action means that the unexpected can be expected from him, that he is able to perform what is infinitely improbable" (Arendt, *The Human Condition,* 178).

117 The term "practical religion" comes from Leach, *Dialectic in Practical Religion.* We might also distinguish between the perspectives of the "expert" and the "man on the street," who may nevertheless be one and the same person, only at different modes of attention (Schutz, "The Well-Informed Citizen").

iting from thinking with metahumans is artificial; in the monotheistic traditions, as Rémi Brague observes, the word G/god "oscillates between its linguistic status as a common noun and its usage, which makes it a proper name."[118] Yet, as the history of theology attests, the question is subject to profound contemplation. Some primary religious texts and theological commentaries describe God as a concept or Word, drawing from the Greek Logos, while others agree with Eastern Orthodox philosopher Christos Yannaras, who affirms that, "We know God by cultivating a relationship, *not* [my emphasis] by understanding a concept."[119]

---

118 Brague, "God," in *The Dictionary of Untranslatables*, 403–4.
119 As quoted on https://lifeondoverbeach.wordpress.com/page/2/, accessed 11 February 2018. In the monotheistic traditions the issue may be described as one of meta-metaperson and meta-concept. For Yannaras, "existence is to be perceived only in persons. One consequence of this is that we cannot properly conceive of God as a 'First Cause,' external to His effects: if He is personal, we must see Him as creative energy relating to creation in the present, establishing communion between Himself and His creatures" (Rowan Williams [former Archbishop of Canterbury], "The Theology of Personhood: A Study of the Thought of Christos Yannaras," *Sobornost* 6, 1972: 415–30 [no page numbers in online version]). And further, "the mode of God's being is personal communion." "One of Yannaras's central concerns is to establish that the relation between God and man is personal and reciprocal, a relation of communion, a 'real' (as opposed to a logical) relation." Conversely, for philosopher Anthony Kenny such anthropomorphism is untenable insofar as an all-knowing and unchanging being could have no memory or intelligence ("Anthropomorphism vs Humanism"). When I asked my colleague Valentina Napolitano, an anthropologist of Roman Catholicism, whether God was better conceived as a concept or a person, she responded decisively, "a force!" (personal communication, 15 May 2018). Compare for ancient Greece: "The gods, however, despite their anthropomorphic appearance, were not persons so much as powers, ordered and classified according to the system of Greek religious thought" (Zaidman and Pantel, *Religion in the Ancient Greek City*, 177, with thanks to Barbara Kowalzig for the source). Such "powers" can only be grasped by means of concepts and figures. See also Lienhardt, note 22 above.

The issue has characteristic manifestations in Christianity,[120] Judaism,[121] and Islam. In Islam, the Word, that is, the Qur'an, has priority, but there is an attraction to the person of Muhammad.

---

120 Where the Old Testament begins with the personal, "God created man in his own image," the New Testament begins with the conceptual, "In the beginning was the Word, and the Word was with God, and the Word was God" (respectively, Genesis 1.27 and The Gospel According to John, 1.1). The Word derives from the Greek concept *logos*, the universal principle or ultimate cause, semantically empty in the hands of the Presocratics but here identified with God become a person. John continues, "And the Word was made flesh, and dwelt among us ... full of grace and truth." In the New International version this is translated as, "The Word became flesh and made his dwelling among us" (John 1.14). Aquinas speaks of the Incarnate Word, while Goethe famously inverts the phrase such that "In the beginning was the deed" (Aquinas, *Summa Theologiae,* np; Goethe, *Faust: Part I,* line 903). Monk argues that Goethe's statement could stand as the motto for Wittgenstein's later philosophy (*Ludwig Wittgenstein,* 579).

121 Responding to what he calls a stereotype concerning whether God or the law is at the centre of Judaism, Rabbi David Hartman says the Word or law embodies the living reality of God (rather than God incarnating the law) ("Judaism as an Interpretive Tradition," 6–7, 3–36, with thanks to Jack Kugelmass for directing me to Hartman). Hartman describes the relationship between God and the Jewish people as one of "intimacy and partnership ... a covenantal model – in which God not only tolerates but demands and delights in Jews' taking of responsibility ... [depicting] a religious anthropology characterized not by slavishness and a howling sense of inadequacy in the face of an infinite commanding God" (*The God Who Hates Lies,* 6). As a placard I recently observed raised by the Jewish community in Warsaw puts it, the Jewish God is "a personal, indivisible, non-material, bodiless and eternal Being." Yet for Hartman's son, anthropomorphizing God is a metaphor, a means for ordinary humans to begin to comprehend something infinite and transcendent. Donniel Hartman cites the Talmudic rabbis (BT Sotah 14a): "Is it possible for a person to walk after God? Behold! It has already been said, 'For the Lord your God is a consuming fire.' Rather, one should follow after the Holy One's characteristics: Just as God clothed the naked ... so shall you clothe the naked. Just as God visited the sick ... so shall you visit the sick ..." He adds, "The rabbis grappled with the question of how finite human beings, confined to the realm of the physical, can be said in any meaningful way to *follow* an infinite, transcendent being ..." (*Putting God Second,* 29).

Indeed, there is conflict in Mayotte, as throughout East Africa, concerning the legitimacy of recitations in his honour. Vita is deeply engaged in their performance, whereas Salim rejects them. More generally, Islam contains a running debate about whether relations with God should be conceived as relatively impersonal and rule-bound or pursued with love, intimacy, and spontaneity.[122]

Anthropologists tend to see metahumans as personifications of the conceptual.[123] Sahlins cites a Telefolmin interlocutor in Papua New Guinea who says of metahumans, "All these names are just names. The true thing is Magalim."[124] So names of diverse metapersons refer here in effect to a single concept, sometimes translated as "law," and such concepts are figured as persons. I once suggested that in precolonial Africa and Madagascar the words later personalized as "God" may have indicated a deictic concept, analogous to a concept like "home," whose substantiality is always context-dependent.[125] If deity is deictic, the question is not whether Malagasy *Ndrañahary* (or Telefol Magalim, etc.) and God are one and the same *person*, as the more open-minded missionaries asserted, but whether they are the same *concept*.

Here is an animist illustration from Viveiros de Castro. If a group of Amerindians say that peccaries are humans this is neither

---

122 See for example, Haeri, *Say What Your Longing Heart Desires*; Ahmed, *What Is Islam?*

123 Thus Philippe Descola describes figuration as "the public instauration of an invisible quality through a speech act or an image … Religion embodies, religion incarnates, religion renders present in visible and tangible manifestations the various alternations of being, the manifold expressions of non-self, and the potencies which contain all their acts" ("Presence, Attachment, Origin," 37). He distinguishes among incarnates as spirits, deities, and predecessors (including ancestors and totems). The concept of the "figure" is itself complex and fascinating, conveying the sense of both image and number, and as a verb, of imagining and solving. It adverts to the distinction of figure and ground and hence the duck/rabbit problem. It relates also to the *"personnage"* of Marcel Mauss and to the concept of the dramatic character within a cast of related figures. See also Barker, Harms, and Lindquist, eds, *Figures of Southeast Asian Modernity*; and Lambek, "Afterword."

124 Sahlins is quoting the ethnographer Dan Jorgensen, "What's in a Name," 352, as cited in Sahlins, "The Original Political Society," 111.

125 Lambek, "Provincializing God?"

because they "believe" it to be the case (and hence the anthropologist must also decide whether to believe) nor because they are speaking metaphorically; it is rather that peccary and human are here "inseparable variations of a single concept." That is, there is a concept that embraces both peccaries and humans, and this concept is not the same, or readily translated, as either "humans" or "peccaries"; it is incommensurable with both these concepts and no doubt with our concept of species.[126]

These questions provoke further discussion that I cannot pursue here. But my position is that person and concept are different aspects of metapersons; asking whether God is exclusively *either* a person *or* a concept is another category mistake. Insofar as we live with metahumans as both concepts and persons, our relations with them cannot be reduced to such things as "belief" or "experience."[127] Earlier I said I was avoiding the term "religion"; perhaps now you can glimpse why.

---

126 Viveiros de Castro, "The Relative Native": "It is not 'first' the peccaries and the humans each in their own place, and 'then' the idea that the peccaries are humans: on the contrary, peccaries, humans, and their relation are all given *together* ... The intellectual narrowness that afflicts anthropology ... consists in reducing the notions of peccary and human merely to a proposition's independent variables, when they should be seen – if we want to take Amerindians seriously – as inseparable variations of a single concept" (494–5). And further: "Hence, when told by his indigenous interlocutors (under conditions that must always be specified) that peccaries are human, the anthropologist should ask herself or himself, not whether or not 'he believes' that they are, but rather what such an idea could show him about indigenous notions of humanity and 'peccarity'... The native is not giving the ethnographer an opinion, he is effectively teaching him what peccaries and humans are, explaining how the human is implied in the peccary" (495). Finally, he adds this twist: "The peccaries are peccaries *and* humans, they are humans inasmuch as humans are *not* peccaries; peccaries imply humans, as an idea, in their very *distance* from them. Thus, to state that peccaries are human is not to identify them with humans, but rather to differentiate them from themselves – and therefore us from ourselves too" (496).
127 That metapersons are both conceptual and personal may help to clarify arguments over "believing in" and "believing that," or "knowing that," shifting between trust in persons and reliance on concepts. See Pouillon, "Remarks on the Verb 'to Believe,'" and Ruel, "Christians as Believers."

8 Conclusion

I've covered a lot of ground and much too quickly.

I have tried to think about and by means of both concepts and persons and to use our relations with one to think about our relations with the other. Salim stands in the lecture not only as himself, having his unique life to lead, and leading it, but also as a kind of metaperson, a figure for anthropology as I practise it.[128] The juxtaposition of concepts with persons also suggests the following analogy: just as we can never get things fully and consistently right with other people – relations being subject to misunderstanding, ambivalence, and competing pulls, minds subject to opacity, acts to infelicities, and practice to incontinence – so we cannot live with concepts consistently, live without exercising practical judgment between them or making category mistakes.

Roy Rappaport begins his great book on ritual by observing that, for all its benefits, human language brings with it uncertainty concerning whether or in what sense any given utterance is true or any speaker reliable.[129] Given our ability to communicate by means that exceed the indexical, we readily fabricate and imagine; things can always be otherwise than what is said. Where Rappaport focuses on lying, I attend to mistakes. I distinguish inadvertent conceptual mistakes (mistakes of grammar) from intentional lies, irrational arguments, and factual errors. If no other animal conceives as well as we do, none misconceives as badly or as regularly, either.[130] A realist account of human life must acknowledge that we do not think and act in the world without making mistakes; indeed,

---

128 I don't pretend to fully understand Salim, and I don't know how he might resolve (or how he has resolved) his dilemma. I think the unconscious plays a role in ways I have not been able to address but that would not (reductively) "explain" his situation.

129 Rappaport, *Ritual and Religion*.

130 Alexander Pope memorably sums up the argument: "In doubt his mind or body to prefer; Born but to die, and reas'ning but to err" (Epistle II of *An Essay on Man*, lines 9–10). Put in hermeneutic terms, if our ontological condition is one of interpreting the world, so interpretation presupposes misinterpretation or mal-interpretation, and the need for understanding presupposes a background or alternative of misunderstanding.

philosophical debate presupposes it. This may seem harsh, but it is only a short step beyond the Socratic wisdom of knowing that we do not know. Moreover, while mistakes can be accompanied by suffering, as they were for Salim, they can also be neutral or positive.

Lévi-Strauss describes thought as a process of commensuration. Signifieds are articulated along axes of similarity and difference, established by the binary features of material signifiers. Such signifiers render commensurable concepts that in the abstract are not.[131] In describing this "science of the concrete," Lévi-Strauss was also thinking by means of similarities and differences. His successors, Descola and Viveiros de Castro, follow suit, setting up axes of difference and similarity to paint brilliant, provocative, holistic pictures.[132] Structuralism offers a powerful mode of ordering, and analogical reason offers a significant alternative to reified abstraction, but they ignore what does not fit, lies outside, or otherwise escapes the structure of relations.[133]

---

131 "The dialectic of superstructure, like that of language, consists in setting up *constitutive units* (which, for this purpose, have to be defined unequivocally, that is by contrasting them in pairs) so as to be able by means of them to elaborate a system which plays the part of a synthesizing operator between ideas and facts, thereby turning the latter into *signs*. The mind thus passes from empirical diversity to conceptual simplicity and then from conceptual simplicity to meaningful synthesis" (Lévi-Strauss, *The Savage Mind*, 131). He speaks also of "a system of concepts embedded in images" (264).

132 Descola, *Beyond Nature and Culture*; Viveiros de Castro, *Cannibal Metaphysics*.

133 Yet as Anne-Christine Taylor observes, in "Distinguishing Ontologies," Descola's is a thought experiment of ideal types, and he recognizes that every society contains elements of his other models, subsisting, presumably incommensurably, alongside one another. Both Mary Douglas, *Purity and Danger*, and Victor Turner, *The Ritual Process*, do explore what is in the interstices and emphasize the productivity of pollution and confusion, but these are defined by the structure itself rather than being simply at odds with or to one side of it. This is explicit in Douglas (dirt is "matter out of place") and true also for models that emphasize the powers of inversion: see Stallybrass and White, *The Politics and Poetics of Transgression*.

Practical judgment or analogical reasoning are needed precisely where alternatives are not, or not immediately, commensurable. This is evident once we turn to thinkers actively thinking, rather than attending only to abstracted or given systems of thought.

To treat incommensurable concepts as though they were commensurable is to simplify, and perhaps oversimplify, conceptual use and judgment. Commensurability frequently places alternatives in relations of either/or. Thinkers may come to find such ostensible binary oppositions as subject/object, poetry/philosophy, social/cultural, and particular/universal indispensable, yet deeply problematic. The issues are heightened with respect to pairs in which one of the concepts posits the two as a unity, while the other concept posits them as distinct. From the perspective of the body, mind and body are unified, whereas from the perspective of mind they are distinct.[134] From the perspective of culture, culture and nature are distinguished as humanity considers its place and distinctiveness in relation to the rest of the world. But from the perspective of nature, they are a whole.[135] Thus Lévi-Strauss argues that the making of (cultural) distinctions is itself a (natural) process of human thought, intrinsic and beyond specific intention.[136] This creates a kind of paradox insofar as both/and includes recursively within it an either/or. This is evident between monism and dualism, where each concept can seem to enfold the other: monism including dualism as part of the whole and dualism characterized as the opposition between itself and monism.[137]

---

134 For the full argument, illustrated by means of spirit possession, see Lambek, "Body and Mind in Mind, Body and Mind in Body,"

135 I would defend continuing use of the nature/culture pair despite critiques of its universality. At the most abstract, the nature/culture dichotomy indexes the human recognition of a gap between language or concepts and world or experience, without giving it any particular content.

136 Lévi-Strauss notoriously wrote that it is "not how men think in myths, but how myths operate in men's minds without their being aware of the fact" (*The Raw and the Cooked*, 12).

137 The trick is to acknowledge and understand the prevalence of *both* dualism and non-dualism in human thought and practice, perhaps even as distinct logical types.

It may be that philosophers have resolved these matters in the abstract, but I suggest they continue to be of concern for practical reason and perhaps intrinsic to our condition.[138] Perhaps they contribute to our sense of the world as remarkable or strange.[139]

To describe the human condition as replete with incommensurability, grammatical non-sense, or error is disquieting, and it is a picture from which any number of programs try to preserve us, whether by means of religious truth, science, logic, or philosophy. Certain disciplines, supported by church, state, or academy, not to mention the machinery of the economy, have the power and interest to impose models of commensurability.[140] In attempting to escape the human world of contingency and error for one of certainty and truth, projects of salvation (or simply Weberian bureaucratic rationalization) are apt to produce further error.[141] A shift from a tacit both/and context to an explicit either/or model is more likely to rest on category mistakes than to resolve them. Exhilarating as they can be, movements to expunge error are prone to create errors more vicious than those they want to overcome.[142]

---

138 It could be argued that for Lévi-Strauss it is precisely the fact that incommensurable differences cannot be resolved (fully mediated, in his language) that generates further attempts at commensuration.

139 See Diamond, "The Importance of Being Human."

140 Such movements of purification are sometimes taken as a feature or product of modernity (Latour, *We Have Never Been Modern*) but are by no means exclusive to it.

141 The very idea of salvation could be mistaken. While I cannot defend the point here, I think that some degree of error is inevitable – we can't think of or describe the world without error – and necessary – cultural edifices must rest on a degree of error, if only one of misrecognition, dependent on what Rappaport (*Ritual and Religion*) calls the mystification of performativeness. For Rappaport this misrecognition of the source of order in human action is actually our only basis for establishing and protecting truth and certainty. As he makes clear, sacred truth of this kind is to be distinguished from logical or correspondence conceptions of truth or lower levels of justification.

142 This is not to say that it cannot be liberating to replace a mistake one has taken for granted with a fresh one. Explicit both/and models are not ideal either. For one thing, insofar as they encapsulate either/or alternatives, they include the source of their own undermining; a salient example is

My point evidently is not that we can or should uproot all mistakes; on the contrary, I suspect the only way to live sanely is to acknowledge their existence and choose our corrections judiciously. Wisdom is not to be equated with logic, and logic is necessary but not sufficient to the world. While we rightly admire and depend on consistency and coherence, we also appreciate the challenge and beauty of incommensurability, irony, and incertitude, much as theologians value paradox or mystery and literary critics value ambiguity.

I am not advocating irrationalism or nihilism.[143] The mistakes in question are *not* ones of contradiction, irrationality, or outright falsity (like denial of climate change), and they are not (directly) ones of injustice; *they are a function of our life with concepts, not with facts.* The rational and the ethical cannot be disarticulated from one another. Using one's concepts, like drawing on one's friends, calls for insight and care. With respect to error, we have to balance vigilance with relaxation and use practical judgment to consider when to point out grammatical mistakes and whether ostensible errors can be redescribed in other terms.

Insofar as humans err, this propensity should be as much the subject of philosophical or anthropological acknowledgment and

---

a model of free speech that enables the propagation of illiberal opinions. For another, insofar as they claim to be both/and on a basis of ostensible commensurability, such comprehensiveness is achieved by denying or concealing disparity. In other words, though appearing or claiming to be a both/and model, they are actually one pole of an either/or that they have not fully acknowledged or imagined. I suggest evolutionary psychology is an example. In other words, another kind of prevalent mistake is describing either/or models as both/and.

143 My position is perhaps akin to that which Simon Critchley attributes to Stanley Cavell, namely that he "is seeking to draw us into a position where we are denied both the possibility of an epistemological guarantee for our beliefs and the possibility of a sceptical escape from those beliefs. Of course, this is hard for us to bear ..." Yet, "The denial of scepticism would ultimately be the denial of what it is to be human" (Critchley, "Cavell's 'Romanticism' and Cavell's Romanticism," 48). I would replace the word "beliefs" with "concepts." Critchley speaks of Cavell's "tragic wisdom." Perhaps this is the best I can offer Salim.

inquiry (and not just correction or therapy) as the fact, say, that we acknowledge the majesty of death. In other words, we should be no more dismissive of human error than we are of any other human activity.[144]

To understand other ways of life requires openness toward them, but treating them seriously and with respect must include acknowledging their vulnerability to error. To do this justly and justifiably means recognizing our own limits and errors – of reason, judgment, tact, prejudice, grammar, consistency, and comprehension – such that our discernment or enunciation of error may itself be an error.

I follow Diamond in suggesting that one of our errors is "the limiting philosophical view of language ... and the idea in it that, if a word has descriptive content at all, that content can be expressed by an evaluatively neutral term. Description itself is thought of as something that can be pulled out of the context of human life and interests within which descriptions have their normal place. Against this," Diamond claims, "the capacity to use a descriptive term is a capacity to participate in the life from which that word comes; and ... what it is to describe is many different kinds of activity."[145] One of these activities is anthropological description of people putting things under description and living with the descriptions they have made or been subject to.

I close with an image of error or intellectual presumption prevalent during my time at Michigan. We learned that the doors to

144 This paragraph is taken from Lambek, "Remarks on Wittgenstein's Remarks on Frazer."

145 Diamond, "Losing Your Concepts," 267. As Jack Sidnell points out (personal communication), and as Diamond acknowledges, similar points can be found in Bernard Williams, *Ethics and the Limits of Philosophy*. Diamond also draws upon Murdoch, "Vision and Choice in Morality"; and Cavell, *The Claim of Reason*, Part 3 (Diamond, "Losing Your Concepts," 263, notes 17 and 18). One consequence of Diamond's argument is that anthropologists need to distinguish the application of descriptive terms internal to the forms of life they study from those internal to the language game of anthropology. In the past this was misdescribed as emic and etic, a distinction that surely exemplifies a category mistake.

Javanese houses had vertical panels built a few feet in front so that one had to go around them to enter. This was to stop demons, who, it was said, could move only in straight lines. This illustrated the demonic hubris of speaking of direct cause and effect and was supposed to persuade us of ecological and cybernetic models.[146]

Despite my own circuitous path today, given what I have said about error, I've surely bumped against many panels. The movement I hope to have emulated is the one by which Geertz describes anthropology as "a continuous dialectical tacking between the most local of local detail and the most global of global structure in such a way as to bring both into simultaneous view."[147] This is to finesse the false opposition between the particular and the universal and perhaps between anthropology and philosophy.

---

146 While recognizing the discrepancy between human meaning and the natural world, Rappaport's project at its grandest was to seek commensuration between the natural and the cultural through the regulation of cybernetic flows (*Ritual and Religion*). If cybernetics describes the flow of information within and between systems, in Rappaport's argument it is informationless utterances and ritual acts that overcome the inadequacies of ordinary discursive language and provide regulation.

147 Geertz, "From the Native's Point of View," 69; "... [O]r can a part contain the whole?" asks Pope (*An Essay on Man*, Epistle I, line 32).

COMMENTARIES

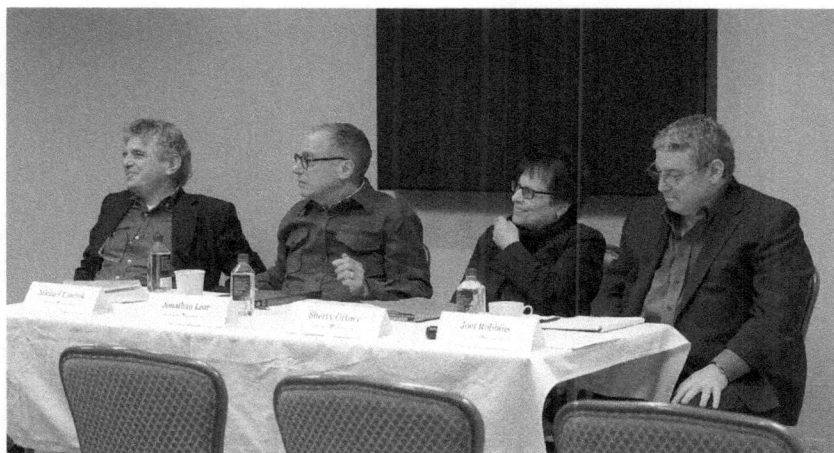

From left to right: Michael Lambek, Jonathan Lear, Sherry Ortner, and Joel Robbins at the University of Michigan on 30 January 2019

Teresa Schmid, Michigan Publishing, University of Michigan Library.

Another Description: Serious Games

SHERRY B. ORTNER

I am thrilled and honoured to be part of this important event with Michael Lambek as the 2019 Tanner Lecturer. Michael was a star among the graduate students in the Department of Anthropology here at the University of Michigan in the 1970s, and I spent years bragging that I had been part of his PhD committee, until he very gently told me that I actually hadn't been. I have recovered from the blow and have continued to admire his work over the years, including the many fine writings that have come out of the stunning extent and depth of his fieldwork in Mayotte.

For his Tanner Lecture, Lambek has presented us with the story of Salim, a young man from Mayotte with a Western education whose mother had performed curing work involving trafficking with spirits. His mother died suddenly, and Salim has great anxiety that the spirits will now try to rise in him. But he views trafficking in these spirits as diabolic, antithetical to his commitment to Islam, and does not want to have anything to do with them. He is tormented by their appearance in his dreams, and tormented as well over not having stopped his mother from her work with the spirits. Where other spirit mediums manage to live effectively with both spirits and Islam, in part by distinguishing between different kinds of spirits, Salim lumps them all together and wants to banish all of them, but for various reasons feels he cannot do that.

Lambek's primary interpretation of Salim's torment is what he calls Salim's "life with concepts" (21). Lambek never specifically defines concepts but, drawing on Cora Diamond, he makes an important distinction between concepts as categories of classification and concepts as – though he never uses this phrase – aspects of "description." The classification point leads into a very interesting discussion of Lévi-Strauss which I won't have time to discuss here. As for concepts as aspects of description, Lambek, again drawing on Diamond, elaborates what we might think of as a practice theory of concepts, in which their meanings emerge from the uses to which they are put in contexts of practical life. These contexts are sometimes specified as "language games" as when, in a footnote, Lambek discusses the spirits bothering Salim: "One could say the terms [for the various spirits] have no external referent or object for which they stand but find their meaning only through use in specific language games" (30, n88).

Lambek's emphasis on the role of concepts produces some compelling interpretations of Salim's quandary, especially when he places Salim's case in a larger historical perspective. In Lambek's interpretation, Salim's problem with spirits stems in part from his inability, or refusal, to distinguish among different kinds of spirits, leaving open the possibility of relationships with some that would not necessarily be antithetical to his religious beliefs. Salim insists, however, that they are all bad, "devils," and he must rid himself of them. Lambek labels this a "category mistake," and goes on to draw a parallel with broader trends toward all-or-nothing religious commitments in reformist Islam and other modernist contexts: "in attempting to live in this manner, Salim joins large numbers of people across the globe ... who see the world in terms of incompatible concepts and mutually exclusive alternatives. To the degree such movements are successful, there is no longer a category error but a new description of the world. However, in this instance, as in many others, the shift remains contested and incomplete, and Salim is caught on the crux" (32).

In that and other parts of Lambek's paper, the view from "concepts" can clearly be quite productive. But I would like to go further with Lambek's point that concepts must be understood as taking their meanings from practical, lived contexts. One kind of context, as noted earlier, is the "language game," drawn from the philosophy of Ludwig Wittgenstein. For present purposes I would like to broaden the game concept beyond language, to include all the kinds of social and cultural games that define the terms in which life is lived and concepts are thought within given times and places. At this point then I need to take a brief excursion through some important usages of the game metaphor in social theory. And although none of the authors will use a language of "concepts," I think you will see the family resemblance to Lambek's discussion.

The metaphor of social life as a game, or a collection of games, has an important history in the social sciences. There is first of all the formalistic and predictive "game theory" of the economists and political scientists which assumes a rational self-maximizing subject. This use of the game metaphor will not play any role in the present discussion, and in fact is quite antithetical to the uses I will discuss, in which the game metaphor is part of an attempt to capture the dynamically interactive, structured but improvisational, and meaning-filled organization and practice of ordinary social life.

Before going on, however, I need to note that I have gotten a good deal of negative reaction in the past for using the game metaphor at all. Perhaps it can work, so the criticism goes, for some of the more positive domains of social life, but what about genocide, racism, capitalist exploitation, patriarchy? Are these not diminished in their terrible seriousness by the use of the very word "game," with its implications of play and fun? This problem surely underlies the fact that all the authors who use some version of the game metaphor modify it with heavy adjectives meant to counterbalance the lightness of associations with games and play. We see a recurrence of oxymorons surrounding the concept: Geertz's (Bentham- inspired) "deep play," Bourdieu's (Plato-inspired) "playful seriousness," and my own (not remembering that Geertz had used the phrase once) "serious games." Here I will focus on Geertz and Bourdieu.

Clifford Geertz uses the game metaphor in several different ways in his work. In a late book, *Available Light* (2000), he traces his interest in the metaphor back to Wittgenstein's "language games," connecting directly with Lambek's discussion. In another context, he uses the phrase "serious games" in discussing some of the work of Erving Goffman. Here he emphasizes, following Goffman, the ways in which seeing social life "as a collection of games means seeing it as a grand plurality of accepted conventions and appropriate procedures – tight, airless worlds of move and counter move, life *en règle."*[1]

But his most famous use of a game metaphor is to be found in his article "Deep Play: Notes on the Balinese Cockfight." Here he emphasizes less the Goffmanesque nature of game playing, of strategic improvisation within a structure of rules, although that is not completely absent, as the players of course must both follow the rules and play to win. More important in this discussion is the argument that participation in deep cultural games shapes and indeed constructs actors' subjectivities: "Enacted and reenacted, so far without end, the cockfight enables the Balinese ... to see a dimension of his own subjectivity ... Yet because ... that subjectivity does not properly exist until it is thus organized, art forms [like the cockfight] generate and regenerate the very subjectivity they pretend only to display."[2] Going on, then, to the most general level, Geertz argues that the games of life, and especially high-stakes games like the Balinese cockfight, construct a sense of the meaningfulness of life itself in the deepest sense: "to the Balinese what [deep play] mainly increases is the meaningfulness of it all. And as ... the imposition of meaning on life is the major end and primary condition of human existence, that access of significance more than compensates for the economic costs involved."[3]

The game metaphor is even more pervasive throughout the work of Pierre Bourdieu, and he too uses it in several different ways. Bourdieu's whole theoretical model of the practice of social life, in which actors improvise within the limits and options of a deeply embedded *habitus*, can be seen as based on the game analogy, although he tends to specifically reserve the "game" word for more limited contexts. He uses literal games, sports, to illustrate the ways in which social life is lived largely intuitively and bodily, not through conscious rule-following but through having "a feel for the game":[4] "A player who is involved and caught up in the

1 Geertz, "Blurred Genres," 26.
2 Geertz, "Deep Play," 450–1.
3 Geertz, "Deep Play," 434.
4 Bourdieu, *The Logic of Practice*, 66.

game adjusts not to what he sees but to what he fore-sees, sees in advance in the directly perceived present; he passes the ball not to the spot where his team-mate is but to the spot he will reach ..."[5]

Like Geertz, Bourdieu is interested in the ways in which involvement in particular games gives rise to particular forms of consciousness. This is especially evident in *Distinction*, where he considers the different worldviews, almost sub-cultures, of the French social classes, arising out of the differing ways in which they play the games of class and status in contemporary French society. But Bourdieu's notion of subjectivity is quite different from Geertz's. For Geertz, what actors internalize through participating in the games of culture is the particular "ethos" of their cultural milieu, a style of being in the world, an arrangement of feelings and understandings. For Bourdieu, on the other hand, actors come to embody a *habitus*, a set of categories, rules, and dispositions oriented toward action or practice. Geertz's actors tend to be shaped as subjects; Bourdieu's subjects tend to be shaped as actors.

Finally, and perhaps surprisingly, Bourdieu, like Geertz, sees the games of life as productive not only of specific cultural meanings (consciousness, subjectivity, *habitus*) but as productive of the very essence of meaning itself. At one point he says, "There is no way out of the game of culture,"[6] suggesting that it is not possible to stop playing the games. But in several contexts he brings up the idea of *illusio* or "belief in the game"[7] and talks about the effects of losing those illusions, that belief: "Indeed, one only has to suspend the commitment to the game ... in order to reduce the world, and the actions performed in it, to absurdity, and to bring up questions about the meaning of the world and existence which people never ask when they are caught up in the game ..."[8] As in Geertz, then, it is life-as-(culturally specific)-games that creates not only the specific forms of our identities and our engagement in the world but

---

5 Bourdieu, *The Logic of Practice*, 81.
6 Bourdieu, *Distinction*, 12.
7 Bourdieu, *Distinction*, 54.
8 Bourdieu, *The Logic of Practice*, 66–7.

the sense of the world as a place of meaning, value, passion, and commitment.

Although neither Geertz nor Bourdieu uses a language of concepts, for both there is a kind of shared model in which participation in the games of life both draws on and produces the stuff that profoundly organizes thought and feeling, whether we call that stuff concepts, or meanings, or categories, or capital-M meaning itself. My point here is that this model is implicit in Lambek's paper as well, though often relegated to footnotes. And so I will close by asking what this games perspective might add to our understanding of Salim's predicament. Lambek's first "description" of Salim's dilemma concerns Salim's problematic relationships with "persons," with both his mother and with the spirits, or what Lambek calls "metapersons." Lambek's second line of description pursues what he calls Salim's life with "concepts," Salim's categorizations of "Islam," "spirits," "devils," and so forth, and the way these things get in each other's way. I am suggesting here that a third level of description would be useful, in which Salim's dilemma is explored through the perspective of his participation in cultural games.

We know from Lambek's descriptions that Salim is engaged in at least three such games, which we might call the game of Western modernity, the game of Muslim piety, and the game of village social relations. Knowing this, and adopting a games perspective, we might start by asking why Salim approached Lambek in the first place. Could this be a move with which most anthropologists are familiar, a move by Salim to establish a privileged relationship with the anthropologist by displaying his competence in English, his familiarity with French literature, and so on? But then he speaks disparagingly of the spirits, whom he views as a threat to his pious Islamic practice and his deeper peace of mind. It thus becomes relevant that there is a third party to the conversation, Vita, a respected practitioner of curing whose work involves trafficking with those very spirits whom Salim is disparaging. Does Salim mean to insult Vita? Is Vita insulted? When Vita later reveals something to Lambek that Salim evidently did not want revealed, was that a kind of retaliation for the insult? Of course, I have no idea about the answer to these questions. My point is simply that seeing the complex interaction between Salim, Vita, and Lambek as one involving various moves in various games opens up a different set of questions from those prompted by the view from "persons" and "concepts."

But we can also turn this discussion around. If one use of the games perspective is to make sense of specific interactions, à la Erving Goffman (e.g., 1956),[9] another is to read "upward" and "outward" from encounters like this, to construct accounts of the wider culture in a given time and place, and over time. Recognizing that Salim is not simply improvising his life out of nothing but is drawing on wider games that have a kind of life of their own in Mayotte and far beyond, we can ask questions about those wider games in the world and how they are, or are not, changing. Lambek gave us a glimpse of this kind of reading in the passage I quoted earlier, to the effect that reformist Islam may be bringing about what he called "a new description of the world." Lambek does not use a language of games here, and religious fundamentalism may be one of those areas where a language of games will not feel right. Then again, it might produce some interesting results.

I am not suggesting that interpretations produced through a games perspective should replace any of the compelling interpretations that Lambek has put forward. Rather I see it as another way of doing what he calls "putting things under description." Switching to a personal voice finally, I want to thank Michael for presenting us with this enormously generative paper, and I look forward to the discussion to follow.

---

9 Goffman, *The Presentation of Self in Everyday Life*.

On Games
A Response to Sherry B. Ortner

The main point of Sherry Ortner's intervention, I think, is to gently point out that if I tacked between the micro-level of Salim's personal dilemma and the macro one of human life with concepts, moving between the personal and the philosophical, I left the middle level, the social, fairly empty. Ortner proposes adding another description, moving from Wittgenstein's concept of language games to conceptions of games in social theory as "part of an attempt to capture the dynamically interactive, structured but improvisational, and meaning-filled organization and practice of ordinary social life." She asks what drawing on the concept of the cultural game could add to my analysis. I briefly take up this invitation to consider what such a redescription might offer and what it might risk.[1]

What is a game? In fact, it is itself a concept that is used in a variety of games, both in practice and in theory, like the one we are playing now. As Ortner shows, anthropologists have drawn on the concept in diverse ways. For Geertz, she says incisively, games shape actors as subjects; for Bourdieu they shape subjects as actors.

---

1 My respect for Sherry Ortner goes back to 1976 when I returned to Michigan from dissertation fieldwork and, to my great benefit, audited her undergraduate lectures in which she paired ethnographies with discussion of theorists (Marx, Durkheim, Weber, and Freud) who had inspired them. It was one of the best courses I have ever attended for the comprehensiveness, lucidity, imagination, and enthusiasm with which Sherry lectured, matched only in my experience by a set of open lectures Anthony Giddens delivered two decades later at the London School of Economics. These qualities are evident in the essays and ethnographic works for which Sherry is famous, as in her comments here.

Wittgenstein used the word "game" to illustrate the concept of family resemblance, such that any two uses of the term may have nothing in common with each other, albeit they each do with other uses. Hence language games themselves only share family resemblances with one another and cannot be defined more specifically. As Jack Canfield remarks, "Definitions or analyses of such terms of art as 'language-game' are of no utility: they will be either circular or inept."[2]

However, as Canfield goes on to say, "The 'game' in language-game points to the fact that speaking occurs in a context of human action and interaction; words derive their meanings from their roles in such patterns of interaction."[3] The concept of the game thus recognizes first that speech is action and that it is social; language games are composed of interpersonal acts of initiation and response. Exceptions, such as portrayed in Stefan Zweig's novella *Chess Story* (or *The Royal Game*), only serve to prove the point.

For Wittgenstein there are rules of play. As Kenneth Burke puts it, "the rules of a game define the nature of the players' 'action' in that game," and the players act "competitively cooperating"

---

2 Canfield, "The Living Language," 166. My thanks to Jack Sidnell for directing me to Canfield.

3 In Wittgenstein's *Blue* and *Brown Books*, the term "language game" "is used to denote an activity involved in the learning of language by children and novices" (Sidnell, *Talk and Practical Epistemology*, 84). In Wittgenstein's later use, as Jack Sidnell observes, "language game is used to describe the entirety of language – language just is a mass of incommensurate, interlocking, and overlapping language games" (*Talk and Practical Epistemology*, 84). The point is less to distinguish individual games than to observe that "it is not simply that language is embedded in the ordinary activities of its users, which it surely is, but moreover that its intelligibility derives from its situated and multifaceted relation to these activities" (*Talk and Practical Epistemology*, 86). For Wittgenstein, any deployment of a word uttered and understood in the stream of daily life "is to participate in one or another of various language games" (Canfield, "Living Language," 173). There are basic language games – like greeting; making, granting, and refusing requests; and asking and answering questions – and more elaborate or technical ones like those characteristic of polite dinner parties or university seminars.

to enact the game as a whole.[4] This describes soccer or chess, but
cooperation could trump competition, as in the game of playing
together as an orchestra or looking at family photographs, and
competition trumps cooperation in the market or in war. A salient
question is whether games are played *with* others, or *against* them.
Or perhaps against chance.[5]

Further questions to ask about games include how risky they
are and what is at stake.[6] How much weight is given to tactics and
strategy? Bourdieu's concepts of improvisation and feel for the
game are superb (one could say Salim lacks a feel for the game of
possession), but it is all too easy to take from both Bourdieu and
Goffman a cynical view. This could develop epistemological twists.
I recall Goffman's giving a lecture at Michigan on giving a lecture
on giving a lecture on giving a lecture … A tour de force, but also a
fall down the rabbit hole.

Alasdair MacIntyre makes a helpful distinction in *After Virtue*
where he discusses not *practice* in the abstract sense, as used by
Ortner or by Bourdieu, but *practices*, hence more akin to games.
He distinguishes between goods internal to a given practice and
goods external to it, and hence specific practices according to
whether they are oriented to internal or external goods.[7] Thus
tennis could be played for the pleasure of playing it, for what
C.B. Macpherson called the exercise of the capacities;[8] or it could
be a punishing regime for losing weight or building fitness; or a

---

4 Burke, *The Rhetoric of Religion*, 39.
5 See Malaby, *Gambling Life*.
6 Also, whether they are played individually or in teams. The University
   of Toronto plays the "rankings" game where we are all supposed to be a
   team in raising the profile and excellence of the institution. At the same
   time, my department plays the enrolment game, trying to attract more
   undergraduate majors and thereby more academic positions from the
   dean, and each member plays the tenure and promotions and international
   recognition games.
7 MacIntyre, *After Virtue*. This is somewhat akin to the means/ends
   distinction itself and to the contrast between virtue ethics and
   consequentialist ethics.
8 Macpherson, *Democratic Theory*.

skill developed to win large amounts of money or fame on a professional circuit. Similar questions could be applied to the game of anthropology or a language game as simple as talk about the weather, as well as to the games in which Salim and his fellows could be said to be engaged. Salim's games, as Ortner describes them, are certainly serious, non-competitive ones with internal goods.[9]

Games, as Ortner suggests after Geertz and Bourdieu, create "not only the specific forms of our identities and our engagement in the world but the sense of the world as a place of meaning, value, passion, and commitment."[10] Perhaps the game in this cultural sense most widely discussed in the anthropological literature, though not often conceived as a game, is the Trobriand *kula*. Descriptions of kula vary with respect to whether the ends or goods are viewed as internal or external. Some external arguments are functionalist, emphasizing the cooperative side: the kula provides the pathway for regional trade of material goods, or perhaps maintains social harmony. Others are instrumentalist, emphasizing the competitive: people participate in kula for prestige or power. The internal argument is that people engage in kula because it is fun, exciting, compelling, or otherwise meaningful – because it is kula ("kula for kula's sake"). Players are constituted simultaneously as subjects and agents. Malinowski's canvas is broad enough to incorporate all of this, and kula is well summed up by Mauss as a "total social fact." Thus, as Ortner suggests, the game is a comprehensive way

---

9 I am not sure whether salvation is better described as an internal or external good of the practice (or game) of Muslim piety.

10 The concept of the game articulates how acts or practices are described, meant, and organized in relation to one another and to specific broader goals. Like that of practice or practices, it certainly contains more life than the concept of the text. Between game and text is Ortner's own concept of cultural scenarios (Ortner, *Sherpas through Their Rituals*). To describe the enactment of cultural scenarios as a game would be to emphasize it as recursively goal-oriented, and we could conceive of society as a conjunction of various recursively goal-oriented activities to reproduce valued scenarios. I have drawn on this extensively, most recently in Lambek, *Island in the Stream*.

to conceive and describe the ethical, aesthetic, and meaningful dimensions of social life intertwined with those of function, power, and interest.[11]

There are also risks to drawing on a concept of the game. Each game of theory of ours that plays with the concept of "game," comes with its own assumptions. Hence there is the question, most evident perhaps in economics or international relations, of how what begins as a metaphor comes to be taken literally and the assumptions embedded in the concept become self-confirming, produce what they claim only to put under description, and determine what we can or cannot see.

Stanley Cavell has shown the problems with drawing the analogy between games and moral practice too closely. While the concept of rules may be applicable to both, this does not imply that morality is rule-governed practice. For one thing, in competitive games, "a player's responsibility for what he does is restricted a priori by the rules of the game, which automatically and conclusively settle how what he does is to be described," whereas in moral life, not only are options wider and responsibility broader, but any given act can be defended either by redescription or by justifications and excuses. "Part of what gives games their special quality – what, one may say, allows them to be practiced and played – is that within them what we must do is (ideally) completely specified and radically marked off from considerations of what we ought to (or should not) do. It is as though within the prosecution of a game, we are set free to concentrate all of our consciousness and energy on the very human quests for utility and style: if the moves and rules

---

11 In contrast to the kula in its heyday, the world today is one in which many people are prevented from playing the games they have expected to play – for example, by having no means sufficient to marry or raise a family, no state in which they can participate as citizens, no tournament of status they could enter, let alone win. They have to invent other means and meanings, other games, not only for livelihood, reproduction, civic participation, or social status, but for inspiration, for projecting and mirroring themselves, for living as if it mattered.

can be taken for granted, then we can give ourselves over totally to doing what will win, and win applause."[12]

A converse risk in describing acts as moves in a game is that we don't take them seriously or perhaps assume that the players do not, at least not outside the game in question. That this is a deep and perhaps irresolvable issue is evident in the tensions within our concepts of acting and performance, each of which carries a double sense of serious consequentiality and mere simulation: the deed itself and its representation, the world and the stage. Perhaps this internal tension in our concepts or terms of description speaks to the fact that insofar as our worlds are socially and performatively constructed they are always vulnerable to demystification or loss of Bourdieu's illusion. If, as Ortner suggests, games create "the sense of the world as a place of meaning, value, passion, and commitment," then what happens when the game breaks down or the frame is broken? What anchors or validates the game?

The tension between values internal and external to a given game or practice and the tension indicated by the double meanings of the verbs "to act" and "to perform" raise significant social and existential questions. If it is the case that our acts and performances as members of society are construed as moves in games, and if our acts and roles are subject to disruption, is there some place outside of games, a place for directly being human? In what respect can we or do we transcend social pretence, or is the claim that we do so another form of pretence or illusion?

Although he does not use the language of the game, these questions are positively addressed in Jonathan Lear's Tanner Lectures on irony.[13] Lear begins by describing pretence in Kierkegaard's

---

12 Cavell's argument is to be found especially in chapter XI of *The Claim of Reason*, where the second quotation is found (page 308). The paragraph as a whole is indebted to Jean-Philippe Narboux's incisive discussion, "Actions and Their Elaboration" (in press), from which the first quotation is taken (draft page 14).

13 Lear, *A Case for Irony*, 10. I take some liberties and risk vulgarizing what is a subtle account.

sense of putting oneself forward or making a claim. Taking up a social role, like that of teacher, is a form of pretence in this sense. Hence, pretence is not necessarily false or pretentious.[14] For Lear, "the possibility of irony arises when a gap opens between pretense as it is made available in a special practice and an aspiration or ideal which, on the one hand is embedded in the pretense – indeed, which expresses what the pretense is all about – but which, on the other hand, seems to transcend the life and the social practice in which that pretense is made. The pretense seems at once to capture and miss the aspiration."[15] Irony, then, is a recognition that the practice itself may not be able to live up to its own aspirations. To revert to the language of the game, it is as if the game were revealed as lacking the ultimate significance or point that led us to invest in learning and playing it in the first place, or else were revealed as having indeed a larger purpose of which we had been unaware: the practice revealed either as merely a game or as more than the game we took it for.

Lear's account of disruption is positive. Rather than describing it in terms of cynicism or anomie, he argues that irony entails "an uncanny experience that the demands of an ideal, value, or identity to which [a person] takes himself to be already committed dramatically transcend the received social understandings."[16] Lear is clear that the Kierkegaardian version of irony that he explicates and defends is not one of mere detachment but of "earnestness and commitment"; it is "detachment from the social pretense in order to facilitate attachment to the more robust version of the ideal."[17] This suggests both the limits and the transcendence of the model of any form of social activity conceived as (only) a game.

---

14 Lear, *A Case for Irony*, 10. In her response, "Thoughts about Irony and Identity," Cora Diamond discusses whether or how this is different from the sort of social identity based largely on appearance, like the dandy, or being *un homme comme il faut*.

15 Lear, *A Case for Irony*, 11.

16 Lear, *A Case for Irony*, 25.

17 Lear, *A Case for Irony*, 38.

Lear emphasizes that the vulnerability to ironic disruption "is an intrinsic aspect of our life with the concepts with which we understand ourselves."[18] We can acknowledge or resist this. I suggest both responses are to be found most evidently in practices that we have called "religious," practices that explicitly attempt to transcend the social and ground it in something outside itself.[19] At a personal level, and with respect to the ethnography at hand, this is evident in Vita's dismissal of superficial observance at the mosque in favour of his devotion to the *Mulidy* and submission to the spirits, and it is evident equally in the high stakes for Salim of attending the mosque and refusing the spirits. Diamond suggests that, "The disagreement about how to live, the disagreement between a questioning ironic mode of thinking and a mode of thinking that rejects the insecurity of irony … is also a disagreement about whether ironic questioning, ironic experience of any kind, does reveal a gap between pretense and a genuinely owned aspiration that transcends the social realm."[20] It is notable that Lear himself ends the discussion with a both/and position: "The issue is not about choosing between two opposing principles but about learning to live well with them both. Resistance to irony is as constitutive of human life as is the ironic impulse. I take it that ironic existence – considered as a human excellence – does not single-mindedly take up the cause of irony, but finds healthy and life-affirming ways of embracing the inevitable resistance to it."[21]

Returning to Mayotte, Ortner suggests three games in which Salim is engaged – what she calls the games of Western modernity, Muslim piety, and village social relations. This is an externally imposed set of descriptions, not how people in Mayotte themselves distinguish their activities. Hence, unlike a dominant concept of the game as something in which you are either in or out at any given

---

18 Lear, *A Case for Irony*, 155.
19 See Rappaport, *Ritual and Religion*, on the grounding of social acts and practices in sacred postulates.
20 Diamond, "Thoughts about Irony and Identity," 151.
21 Lear, *A Case for Irony*, 163.

time, these games overlap, blend into, interrupt, and encompass each other in complex ways, with lots of conflicting local opinion about how acts and goals should be articulated, as well as how they are in fact articulated in practice and at what level of generality or inclusion. Hence, if I describe my game as observing people putting things under description with respect to the concept of games, their acts of description are both moves in particular games *and* claims about which game is being played when. Salim's dilemma here could lie in knowing which game he is most committed to and how to put that commitment under subjectively satisfactory description.

Following the rules of the game in Goffman's or Bourdieu's sense, or the grammar of the game, in Wittgenstein's, is where mistakes enter, as well as in mistaking one game for another. There is the question how people move between games, disrupting one line of play for another, and also whether various games are incommensurable with one another, hence with no fixed criteria for choosing between them or knowing which game one is playing at any given moment. We have to acknowledge confusion, interruption, playing badly or distractedly, as well as the ability to play multiple games adeptly at once, having a feel not simply for the game, as Bourdieu puts it, but a feel for playing multiple games simultaneously or alternately.

With respect to the more specific questions Ortner asks about Salim playing games to which Vita and I are drawn in as players, I see the situation much as Lear puts it in his commentary (below). Salim was intellectually curious to meet me. He was strong, serious, and not trying to play us.[22] I don't think Salim intentionally hid the destruction of the money and clothing from me; these matters were simply not relevant to what he wanted to convey. Vita was recovering from a serious medical intervention and probably enjoyed just sitting where he was, under a tree by the beach. As a healer, he had a genuine curiosity about other people. Vita was not insulted, but he predicted that he could become insulted if he took on the case.

---

22 It is also significant that he cut off our conversation at a certain point and did not follow up the invitation to come and see me again.

To describe Salim's action as a game also risks ignoring the fact that Salim sees himself as a kind of pawn in a game the spirits are playing. That is to say that, if games imply active players, we have to see also how players are themselves "played," whether by other players in this or a meta-game, or by structural forces – how, as Ortner puts it, they are constituted as subjects as well as actors. One thing spirit possession has taught me is that agency is complemented by patiency, action by passion.

Finally, a non-cynical concept of the game that may lie at the heart of Wittgenstein's view and of our life with concepts is the game as riddle. This emerges from what Stephen Mulhall describes as "the inherent beyondness of words to themselves, their essential non-self-identity."[23] In particular, suggest Diamond and Mulhall, talk about God might occur only in the form of the riddle.[24] This might describe the game in which Salim most saliently finds himself.

---

23 Mulhall, *The Great Riddle*, 79.

24 "Religious language is thus essentially self-subverting language; the repeated collapse of its affirmations into complete disorder *is* its mode of order – it is, one might say, the only way the 'language-games' woven into transparent religious language-games should be played" (Mulhall, *The Great Riddle*, 59–60). One could also speak simply about the riddle of existence, of who we are as an individual or as a species, or about puzzling out answers to Kant's three questions: What can I know? What should I do? What may I hope for?

Brief Encounter

JONATHAN LEAR

1. "Paradoxically," Michael Lambek tells us in this thought-provoking lecture, "I am making central to my argument someone I barely know" (16). He tells us of a brief encounter with a young man on the island of Mayotte in June 2015. This was Lambek's eleventh trip to the island (8), so it is likely he is well known within the community. In any case, towards the end of his last visit, as he describes it, "as I was chatting with an old friend, Vita, we were approached by an earnest young man, perhaps in his late twenties who declared he had long wanted to meet me" (13). Salim tells Lambek his story, and that was their one and only meeting. Clearly this was a memorable encounter, at least, for the anthropologist; for years later, on the occasion of being invited to give these Tanner Lectures on Human Values, it is this meeting with Salim that Lambek chooses to think through one more time and present to us. To do so he had to overcome his own misgivings. As he says of his presentation in a footnote: "This rubs against my ethnographic practice, which is one of revisiting and conversing with interlocutors multiple times, fully talking through their ideas, and also talking with their consociates" (16, n43). This fascinates me: that in spite of some reluctance, Lambek wants to tell Salim's story anyway. There is something about the figure of Salim that intrigues him; and this Tanner Lecture is his attempt to make sense of their meeting. It is a testament to the wondrousness of human beings that, on a single brief meeting, powerful currents can be established between two people; and a person's imagination can be triggered in such a way that he ends up thinking about the encounter, trying to make something of it, for the rest of his life.

So, in June 2015 Salim comes up to Lambek in the (for us) far-off island of Mayotte and tells him his story. And in January 2019, now, Lambek, comes to us, and retells that story. So, we, the audience and readers, are in some kind of repetition. The story has continued its journey across oceans and continents, through time and space; and now it is here before us. A story depends for its existence on those who hear or read it becoming its bearers, on their continuing to discuss and repeat it. I take my position to be somewhat more intense than yours: for in the designated role of commentator, it is as though Lambek has come up to me and told me his story of someone coming up to him and telling him his story; and now I am called upon to say something. What a remarkable ritual in which I have somehow gotten myself entangled! I wish I understood the ritual better, but I certainly know this much about it: it is my turn.

Commenting on the brevity of his meeting, Lambek says, "We might think of the situation as analogous to understanding a character in fiction in that there are limits to what the writer tells us" (16). I would like to do just that. In talking about "Salim" I am not trying to get to the truth about the actual individual Lambek met who, by now, is in his thirties, who might still be on the island of Mayotte or, for all we know, is studying at the Sorbonne or, indeed, at the University of Chicago. I am going to work with the figure of Salim as presented to us in Michael Lambek's fascinating story, presented to us here as a Tanner Lecture. I am trying to understand better not the actual individual Salim, to whom I have had little exposure, but rather the lives we all live together – especially now that many of us can travel to far-off places, hear and retell other people's stories; and so many of us live in social environments full of people from multiple cultural backgrounds. Here I am taking the "we" to apply as broadly as it legitimately does.

2. I would like to begin with first impressions before going on to a more theoretical discussion. My first thought on reading Lambek's story was that I don't have to travel that far to hear a story like it. If I went into a Hyde Park bar by myself and sat at the bar – or got into a taxi and started talking with the driver – who knows what I might hear? Chicago is such a culturally, ethnically, socially, economically diverse city, with generations of immigrants coming

and, in spite of everything, still coming from all over the world –
many of whom are bearers of traditional cultures, and many of
whom carry within them multiple traditions – it would be surpris-
ing if a story like Salim's is ever very far away. One needs only the
good fortune that one happens to encounter such a person who is
willing to speak his story out loud. And one must, as Lambek was,
be willing to listen.

My second thought was that Salim's mother reminds me of my
own. There are, of course, cultural differences; and no doubt the
concepts Salim's mother used do not translate that well into those
my mother used. For me, the most significant cultural difference
is that, in the suburban world of 1950s New England, there was
no way for my mother to earn a living dealing with spirits and
devils. My mother's psychoanalyst thought these spirits were figures of her imagination, "fantasies" he called them. That was all
the evidence my mother needed to know that the analyst himself
was a demon. When my mother threw my sister, then fifteen, out
of the house for being "a witch" there was a spiritual adviser who
had come from somewhere in India living in the house. He was
teaching her the ways of another culture.[1] For all I know he was
teaching her concepts and ways of living with them that were not
all that different from those used by Salim's mother. Who knows
the transmission?

The point I want to make is that if my mother had died when
I was in my twenties – at Salim's age when his mother died – I
would have been in trouble: psychological trouble, social trouble,
spiritual trouble. Trouble not wildly unlike the trouble Lambek
reports about Salim. Ironically, one of the healthy things I did in
that period is not unlike what Salim did: I found an older man of
some professional substance and told him my story.

---

1 When I showed my sister this comment to get her permission to mention
her, she made this emendation: She was thrown out for being a witch who
had put a curse on the ashram. "Ashram" was how my mother in that
period referred to our home. My sister believes that, if she had been a good
witch, she would have been most welcome to stay. Indeed, in that case our
mother would have been proud of her and wanted her company.

Though it did not always seem so at the time, I had the good fortune to have a mother who lived to a ripe old age. Here are descriptions of what happened to her in her eighties: bad spirits left her,
and good spirits took up residence; she got bored with being angry;
her hormone levels changed; there was a shift in her neurological
structure. I find each of these accounts compelling, but only in conjunction with the others. The upshot was that she became incred-
ibly grateful. A blade of grass, a bird's song, a toddler toddling
would fill her with joy. She lived in Santa Fe, and it would happen
that a Native American selling his wares would, after a conversation with my mother, pull me aside and ask me if I understood
what a spiritual person she was. When, at her request, her children
let her ashes flow into the Rio Grande, they momentarily took on
the shape of a grey ghost and then – *poof!* – the ghost disappeared.
The river gods had accepted her back; at least, so it seemed to me.
I had a sense of completion then, and it has stayed with me ever
since. None of this would have been available to me at Salim's age.

When I read Lambek's rich account of Salim's relation to his
mother, the most salient fact is that she died "recently" "with no
prior warning," and her death "shocked him" (14). It is, I think,
too soon to tell with any confidence what is going on with Salim –
beyond, that is, what he can tell us (and did tell Lambek) about
himself. Customs and rituals after the death of a relative or loved
one differ across time and cultures, and it is important to track
these differences. Nevertheless, there are two broad-scale features
of mourning that apply widely and, I think, are applicable to this
discussion. First, we are not surprised if a person in mourning
expresses a range of emotions – especially circling around grief –
and has a variety of experiences – for example, hearing the voice
and seeing a visual image of the deceased loved one – that, *in other
circumstances*, notably daily life, would strike us as odd, worrying, perhaps pathological. As we know, rituals in certain cultures
encourage displays of emotion, grief, and experience that in other
circumstances would be considered excessive. We also are not
surprised if the mourner is anxious about what I shall loosely call
unfinished business with the loved one. Not just whether the personal relation between the two has been left incomplete, dangling,
bruised, or wounded; but whether there is taint, objective guilt, an

unwelcome legacy, restless ghosts, angry spirits with which one is *landed*, whether one likes it or not. We expect different cultures, different peoples, different individuals to use different formulations, and we expect the formulations to express real differences. Still, it is possible to see commonalities and family resemblances within this range.

Second, we expect mourning in this pronounced form to be transient. A person's life may be transformed forever by his relation with the now-deceased loved one; he may love her and remember her every moment for the rest of his life; his personality may change in significant ways in response to her death. He may, for instance, become more like her. Yet we expect the period of pronounced mourning to be of (indeterminate) finite length. It is a condition from which one eventually emerges. Indeed, mourning rituals of many cultures are structured so as to facilitate this process. Mourning is widely accepted as an integral part of human life. It takes various forms, but generally speaking, it is a socially recognized and accepted way in which we come to terms with the dead, those about whom we care. Actually, a bit more than that. Our sense of the importance of mourning is based on more than empirical generalizations, it is based on a shared sense that mourning those we love is a good thing to do. We take mourning to be important because it is part of our conception, however implicit, of human health and well-being.[2] On one end of the spectrum, we take there to be something amiss if a person is indifferent to the death of someone we thought they loved. There may be myriad explanations, but a person's indifference raises the question whether we had misjudged the significance of the relationship. At the other end of the spectrum, we take it to be not just unusual or interesting but pathological if intense mourning is interminable, if a person is never able to emerge from it. Mourning is thus linked to a normative conception of human well-being – though, again, the details of the norms may differ across cultures and time. This seems to me one area for valuable philosophical thinking and anthropological

---

2 Thompson, *Life and Action*.

research: why should mourning be considered part of what it is for humans to live well?

These two broad-scale features of mourning – accepting a broader range of experience, but expecting the expression of such grief to be transient – have an important consequence. For a wide range of behaviour, emotions, beliefs, and other experiences on the part of the mourner, we should leave in abeyance judgment about whether the expression of grief is pathological. Indeed, there is (and should be) a defeasible presumption of health: that this is how a person is finding an effective way to grieve. There will be exceptions: behaviour so extreme and threatening – to self and others – that we feel confident about intervening in the moment (again, judgments about what these moments are will differ across time and cultures). But a wide range of experiences are accepted as a normal part of mourning that would not be regarded as normal in ordinary daily life. That is part of what mourning is all about – to give space for rich and complex experiences of living with the dead. That means that, for a wide range of experiences, it is only later that we might legitimately be in a position to look back and judge behaviour. If a person is unable to emerge from extreme mourning, we might want to revise our judgment of how things were for her earlier.

The upshot of these reflections is that, based on the encounter Lambek describes, it is premature to offer any diagnosis or normative judgment about how well or badly Salim is doing as he attempts to come to grips with the death of his mother. Lambek tells us that Salim was "stricken at the sudden loss of his mother." But to call his suffering a "tragedy" seems unjustified, given what we know, unless Lambek is using "tragedy" in a loose sense to mean a very sad event. And it seems too soon to go on to say that Salim's reaction represents "a failure to acknowledge his mother's separateness" and equally a failure "to fully acknowledge his *connectedness* to his mother" (18). I do not see evidence in the moment to judge any failure at all. Salim is troubled, but for all we know in the moment this could be part of a marvellous process of acknowledging loss, separation, and connectedness. We would need to know more about how the process extends over time and what form it comes to take.

Again, it is too much to know in the moment, but one should, I think, be open to the conjecture that Salim's approaching Lambek is a sign of creativity, innovation, and resourcefulness. He is willing to talk about his troubles. He asks for help. And he chooses someone who (it is reasonable to suppose) appears professional and sane, someone who sympathetically understands the various worlds in which Salim participates but who at the same time maintains some distance from them all. Salim might have seen Lambek as a well-known "expert" who visits this community from time to time; he might thus have seen this visit as an opportunity he needed to seize. If this were so, Salim's approach would be a remarkable expression of hopefulness on his part.

(If I may be allowed a psychoanalytic parenthesis: this paragraph is addressed to those of you who are interested in psychoanalytic thinking. One of the most significant psychoanalytic discoveries of the past century is that boundaries between self and others, self and world, are a psychological and social development.[3] As such, they are malleable, and so we should expect them to vary – across cultures, but also across individuals within a culture and even for a single individual within the course of a life. From a psychoanalytic perspective, one of the ways people influence us is through fantasies of their taking up residence in our psyches. These fantasies can be efficacious in shaping our own personalities. I cannot here discuss the non-rational mental tropisms – notably, projective identification, introjection, and internalization – that psychoanalysts invoke to understand how these internal figures are established.[4] But we can at least raise the question: How much of this imaginative activity is too much?

---

3   The literature is vast, but see Winnicott, *Playing and Reality*; and Loewald, "On Internalization," "Ego-Organization and Defense," "Primary Process, Secondary Process and Language," "The Therapeutic Action of Psychoanalysis," and "Internalization, Separation, Mourning and the Superego," in *The Essential Loewald*.

4   The literature is again vast, but see Spillius and O'Shaughnessy, eds, *The Writings of Melanie Klein*; Spillius and O'Shaughnessy, eds, *Projective Identification*; and Segal, *Introduction to the Work of Melanie Klein*.

There is no easy answer to this question – and again one should expect answers to vary across cultures. One should also expect answers to vary for a given individual at different times in that person's life. If within a broadly psychoanalytic context someone were to approach me with the kinds of concerns Salim expressed to Lambek, I would wonder whether that person was concerned that his *internal* mother was getting too lively. I would not be surprised if a person's internal mother got busy at the moment the external mother dies. I would be wondering what the person is going to do about it. Salim, as Lambek reports him, seeks help. That for me would stand out: the effort to break out of a closed-off fantasy world with only him and his mother as participants. My preliminary, defeasible thought would be that this looks pretty healthy, robust.)

Lambek continues: "The situation is doubly intractable because Salim has a foot in more than one world, one that advocates autonomy, the other relationality" (18). This claim also seems to me premature. For all we know in the moment, the *apparent* conflicts between Salim's entanglements in the traditional spirit world of his mother and his commitments to Islam may be a source of tractability in Salim's development. Here is another arena for philosophical and anthropological reflection: how are we to understand the difference between merely apparent conflicts in living a life that, as Lambek puts it, "has a foot in more than one world" and real conflicts in living that life? We need to rely on more than the fact that a fundamental text in one area of belief, religion, or culture makes claims that conflict with or even forbid the beliefs and practices of another. It has become an ever-more-familiar aspect of life around the globe that many of us are inheritors of and bearers of multiple traditions. Some may nominally conflict in various ways but need not, on their own, disrupt the living of a resourceful, relatively happy, flourishing human life. We need to reflect more on what constitutes a life or even *a life well lived*. I take it there are ways of living well with apparent contradictions; and so we should not settle for any dogmatic presuppositions about what the unity of a human life consists in. This seems to me a philosophically and anthropologically fruitful arena in which to deploy irony in considering what it is to live a life.

It is importantly true, as Lambek points out, that this account of the problem – as having a "foot in more than one world" – is Salim's own. How can he be a good Muslim and deal with his mother's "devils"? As Salim's self-understanding, it should be given significant weight. Nevertheless, it is interpretively valuable to hold open the possibility that Salim is deploying his self-understanding for defensive purposes. So, to take one imaginative example, perhaps instead of being troubled by the conflicts involved in having a foot in different worlds, Salim is overwhelmed by the terror of living within one world – the traditional spirit-"devil" world of his mother – and he tries to flee that terror and contain it by attributing the problem to conflict between different worlds. Perhaps it is from this terror that Salim collapses the traditional distinction Lambek sets out between *sheitwan*, the "immoral, diffuse and relatively impersonal" beings "who tempt us into misdeeds," and the "amoral beings called *djinn, lulu*, or sometimes also *sheitwan*, with whom one can establish positive personal relations" (30). Perhaps Salim cannot face up to the differences. Who knows? In the moment we cannot adjudicate between different interpretive possibilities. But even more important – and this gets to the fundamental question Lambek is raising in his Tanner Lecture, namely, "How are we to understand persons in their lives with concepts?" – as soon as persons are able to use concepts to conceptualize themselves as being or acting in a certain way, they have the opportunity to use those very concepts to mislead themselves about who they are and what is bothering them. It is precisely this conceptualized form of self-consciousness that makes motivated self-misunderstanding possible. The idea that one suffers from having a "foot in more than one world" is a readily available trope. As interpreters we ought to hold open the possibility that Salim's self-understanding is a motivated confusion, however sincere he is.

3. I would now like to comment on the difficulty of reality. Lambek turns for inspiration to a remarkable essay by the philosopher Cora Diamond, "The Difficulty of Reality and the Difficulty of Philosophy." He understands Salim in these terms:

> Salim suffers what Cora Diamond calls a difficulty of reality, [and quoting Diamond] "the apparent resistance by reality to one's

ordinary mode of life, including one's ordinary modes of thinking: to appreciate the difficulty is to feel oneself being shouldered out of how one thinks, how one is apparently supposed to think, or to have a sense of the inability of thought to encompass what it is attempting to reach. Such appreciation may involve … profound isolation …" (21)[5]

By now you will not be surprised to hear me say that we do not yet know enough about Salim to know whether he suffers this difficulty. But I want to concentrate on something else. It seems to me difficult to understand what this phrase *the difficulty of reality* means, let alone whether it applies to someone. For Diamond is deploying the phrase in a special sense. To understand her one needs to grasp this irony: there are many difficulties of reality one might suffer without suffering the difficulty of reality (in Diamond's sense).

In the above quotation Diamond says that to appreciate the difficulty of reality (in her sense) is "to feel oneself being *shouldered out* of how one thinks." It is not perspicuous what this phrase, *shoulder out*, means. If one takes it simply to be a way of describing a person's self-conscious disturbance with their own thinking – for instance, the experience of conflict that arises from having allegiances to more than one tradition, "a foot in more than one world" – we are likely to miss what Diamond means by the difficulty of reality. Diamond takes the expression "shoulder out" from a poem by Ted Hughes, "Six Young Men," and she uses that poem to explicate what she means by the difficulty of reality. In the poem the speaker is regarding a photograph of six smiling young men, taken forty years earlier. Six months after the photo was taken all of them were dead, killed in the opening phase of World War I. It is beyond the scope of this comment to discuss the poem or Diamond's treatment of it it in any detail.[6] But the crucial issue for Diamond is that the poet is not primarily focused on the psychological difficulties involved in finding reality harsh, cruel, and tough to take, but rather on *reality itself*

---

5 Lambek's quotation of Diamond is from Cora Diamond, "The Difficulty of Reality and the Difficulty of Philosophy," 12.
6 But see Jonathan Lear "The Difficulty of Reality and a Revolt against Mourning."

being difficult. There are, as the poet puts it, "contradictory permanent horrors here."Clearly, there is tremendous psychological suffering involved; but the emphasis is not on the *psychological* difficulty of the experience, but rather on the experience of the difficulty.

There are two important points to note. First, one cannot distinguish the difficulty of reality in Diamond's sense by the amount of pain or suffering involved. There might, for example, be parents who, regarding a photo of their long-dead son, are overwhelmed with grief and anguish. Yet for them, in all their pain, the world holds firm. They know they are regarding a photograph taken long ago; they know their son is long dead; they know he died a horrible death; and they cannot get over it. For them, the world has its horrors, and they suffer grievously from them, but they do not experience the difficulty of reality in Diamond's sense. And yet another couple in similar circumstances of loss and also suffering grievously may well be experiencing the difficulty of reality: experiencing the *contradictory, permanent horrors here.* This is, as Diamond puts it (not quoted by Lambek), "an experience of the mind's not being able to encompass something it encounters."[7] It is an experience not of *a* mind's inability but of *the* mind's inability. This is an experience of the difficulty *of reality* (in Diamond's sense) – and it gives us her sense of being shouldered out. If we consider these two imaginary couples, it should be clear that if we were to encounter them in any brief compass, we would not be able to distinguish who, if anyone, was experiencing the difficulty of reality and who was not. I shall discuss momentarily the challenges this poses for us.

Second, the experience of the difficulty of reality as described in the poem erupts in the midst of what, but for this eruption, might well have been an unconflicted experience of everyday life. It is not about psychological conflicts that might arise from living with concepts from different traditions. Looking at old photographs is something we do. It is a familiar part of everyday life. We are interested in the photographs of those whom we know are now dead: we make trips to museums to see them; we save them in boxes at

---

7 Diamond, "The Difficulty of Reality," 2.

home. They were once living, just as we are now living; but now they are not. This is one of the myriad ways we orient ourselves in time. It is one of myriad ways in which we establish what it is for us to have a past. It is one of the ways we familiarize ourselves with the distinction between the living and the dead. For most of our lives, *in their everyday versions*, the distinction between past and present is unproblematic, as is the distinction between alive and dead. It is precisely these unproblematic distinctions that become problematic in the experience of the difficulty of reality. That is one reason why the experience of difficulty can be so isolating. "What is the problem?" one can hear those around him saying: "People go to war," "some die young," it's a "tragedy." From the point of view of the person experiencing the difficulty of reality, these are clichés: ways of living with concepts that, in the name of understanding reality, *keep us from grasping* its contradictory horrors. The concepts are getting in the way of making intelligible that which they purport to conceptualize.

Now Lambek might be correct that Salim was suffering the difficulty of reality in Diamond's sense, but I do not see the evidence to justify that characterization as opposed to other more familiar formulations: for example, that he was suffering "the difficulty of reality" in the sense of intense mourning of a loved one, or that he was experiencing the pain of psychological conflict that arises when one has internalized commitments to different traditions that, on occasion, do not fit well together. The experience of the "difficulty of reality" in this sense does not itself qualify as an experience of the difficulty of reality in Diamond's sense.

4. Let me conclude with a brief comment on the responsibilities we inherit as philosophers and as anthropologists by recognizing the difficulty of reality in Diamond's sense. Her paper is titled "The Difficulty of Reality and the Difficulty of Philosophy" – and the word "and" is serving as more than a mere conjunction. It is not simply that philosophy is a difficult subject. If philosophy is to live up to its own aspiration – to be an appropriate form of response to difficulties of reality – then as a different register of difficulty comes into view, philosophy needs to be sensitive and vigilant, self-conscious and critical about how to face up to it. Diamond, following Cavell, calls responding well to this challenge "acknowledgment" – though

it is important to recognize that there should be no preconceived assumptions about what acknowledgment consists in. Acknowledgment consists in part in coming to an appropriate understanding of what acknowledgment is. Failure to acknowledge may be a refusal or avoidance or flight from the difficulties of reality. It is in this light that I stand before you trepidatious as a commentator for a Tanner Lecture. A good chunk of Cora Diamond's article examines the failure of previous commentators on a Tanner Lecture – John Coetzee's "Lives of Animals" – to face up to the difficulty he was raising precisely by deploying familiar forms of academic philosophical writing. Their attempts to comment upon the lecture are exhibited by Diamond as forms of avoidance. To put it mildly, I would rather not repeat that failure here.

I am, of course, not an anthropologist, and I do not have an insider's knowledge; but I think we owe Michael Lambek a debt of gratitude for bringing to our attention that a similar challenge faces anthropology. Here is one way to accept that challenge: rather than think about Salim's life with concepts, let us think about our own. How, after all, did Michael Lambek manage to get to Mayotte? I expect he took a plane and a boat; but a better answer is: *he aspired to be an anthropologist*. It is only because of this aspiration – this "value" – that he bothered to take those planes and boats, again and again. In effect, he hitched a ride on his ego ideal. His self-understanding as an anthropologist influenced how he understood his conversation with Salim, and it helped him frame and present this Tanner Lecture. This is life with a concept, in this case, the concept *anthropology*.

So the question is: how well (or badly) does the concept of anthropology – or, in my case, the concept of philosophy – equip us – that is, we who have tried to internalize the norms and values of inquiry, we who aspire to be anthropologists or philosophers – to face up to or acknowledge the difficulty of reality when that difficulty comes into our midst? One of Diamond's points is that contemporary social configurations of academic philosophy – including the Tanner Lecture on Human Values – can so shape a practitioner's self-understanding and identifications that he or she avoids the task of facing up to the difficulty of reality in the name of facing up to it. But, if I understand Diamond correctly, this is only one step on her journey. Part of why I love her article – indeed, why I have come to love her – is that she does not just settle for the critique of others. She is trying to live the concept *philosophy* in an adequate way – and her life with concepts is a reanimation of philosophical activity. Her article is in effect an invitation to join her.

I mention the Tanner Lectures because Diamond discusses them as an instance of failure, but also because here we are. I am so impressed by the generosity of the philanthropic spirit of those who endowed these lectures, and I want to express a heartfelt thank you. And yet I am a tad suspicious of the phrase "on human values." Although nothing is necessitated, I wonder whether the title can encourage the view that our job is to rigorously, objectively consider different values, as though they are independent entities, and perhaps evaluate them. And to what extent does that view encourage us to think our task is to observe values over there, in the lives of other people we can study according to accepted research techniques? Does such a conception facilitate avoidance of reality, in Diamond's sense? What if these were called "The Tanner Lectures on Ethical Problems I Might Be Entangled in Without Realizing It"? How different would the lectures be?

So, to return to anthropology: How well did the concept *anthropology* – as alive in the culture, but also as alive in Michael Lambek's identifications and self-understandings – equip him to deal with a young man who came up to him on the island of Mayotte and asked for help? What if that person *were* suffering the difficulty of reality? My question is not about Lambek or Salim per se; it is about the life of the concept *anthropology*. Does the concept as it is now lived help us acknowledge that difficulty should it arise in our midst, or does it unwittingly encourage us to avoid it?

I do not think it controversial to say that the discipline of anthropology has a chequered history. One cannot tell the history fully without an account of its entanglements in empire and colonialism. And one cannot give an account of how those entanglements became possible without a historical account of the concept of anthropology: in particular, how the anthropologists of the time conceived of themselves and what they took to be legitimate anthropological inquiry. As is well known, the discipline of anthropology has been subject to significant critiques and revisions over the past two generations – much of it carried out by anthropologists them-selves. Speaking as an outsider, this seems a special time to be an anthropologist precisely because the question is again alive how one is to live with the concept *anthropology* in ethically responsive and responsible ways. There are of course challenges: in particular, that the mere fact of reflection and critique does not guarantee that one is free of unconscious transmission of historical taint. Still, this is a challenge that should be invigorating, not cause for defeatist gloom.

It is, I think a major accomplishment of Michael Lambek's rich lecture to help us recognize that the difficulty of reality implies that there is a difficulty of anthropology as well as a difficulty of philoso-phy. And, in closing, it crosses my mind to wonder whether all these difficulties might be addressed by us, philosophers and anthro-pologists working together, by returning to – and reanimating – a common historical root: the desire to give a *logos* of *anthropos*. What would it be to do that adequately?

Premature Interpretation and the Difficulty of Anthropology

A Response to Jonathan Lear

To sum up Jonathan Lear's thoughtful response in a single phrase, I have committed the sin of premature interpretation. Premature because I don't know Salim well enough, and premature because his life is ongoing and he surely will move forward.[1] I have in effect frozen him in the frozen state in which he describes himself. The questions, I wonder, are whether Lear is suggesting first, that I am guilty of poor ethical judgment, and second, whether my lecture indexes a failing, or at least difficulty, of anthropology writ large. *How should we acknowledge that our interpretations are always premature?*

Lear's comments can be divided into two sets, the former coming more as psychoanalyst and the latter more as philosopher.[2] Both are exceptionally lucid and help me clarify some of my assumptions. But I find the first set easier to respond to than the second.

Lear apologizes for offering what he calls a "psychoanalytic parenthesis," but actually this sensibility pervades his comments, culminating in the suggestion that "Salim is deploying his self-understanding for defensive purposes." He says, "we ought to hold

---

1   One of my larger goals beyond this lecture is precisely to think about the lives of people I have known over time and to describe possession as an art of living (Lambek, *Island in the Stream*). Like any life writing, the forward movement is necessarily enacted from the past.

2   Lear is both philosopher and psychoanalyst, and each perspective influences the other. I have been deeply enlightened by his intersections of Aristotle and Freud and his deliberations on irony and heartened by his defence of psychoanalysis in the face of the Crews craze, not to mention *Radical Hope*, which has already become an anthropological classic.

open the possibility that Salim's self-understanding is a motivated confusion, however sincere he is." I am sympathetic to the judgment that I have rushed to describe Salim too quickly, but also grateful for this psychoanalytic description (diagnosis, hypothesis, interpretation) that I could not have discerned myself. The key word here is "motivated."

Lear takes Salim as the figure rather than as part of the ground of the lecture. He asks why I would want to tell Salim's story if I barely knew him, and suggests it is my story, not Salim's that may be at issue. Whatever else we could say about my story,[3] I was less concerned with getting to Salim's unconscious motivations, a subject beyond my competence, than in drawing on him to illustrate broader points about our life with concepts, about incommensurability and category mistakes that anthropology has typically ignored.[4] Hence I appreciate the way Lear takes my story of Salim's story as a story about what anthropology is or might be, or cannot be, and also a story of all of us, a story of a life that is also a story of "the lives we all live together," or one in which, as Stanley Cavell puts it, "Each life is exemplary of all, a parable of each; that is humanity's commonness, which is internal to its endless denials of commonness."[5]

As Lear says, one need not travel far to find interesting stories. But that is no reason to ignore distant places. There are at least two well-rehearsed reasons to seek stories abroad; first, some of the stories might show us that people at a distance are not so different from us as prejudice or ignorance might have it;

---

3 At a conscious level, for me the exchange with Salim somehow validated my presence and stood as an index of a major change in Mayotte; it summed up continuous processes in one sharp encounter. And it marked a transformation not just in Mayotte but in my relationships with people there, changes that are also a subject of a broader discussion within anthropology about itself. You could say I should have known already some of what I learned that day. And perhaps I did, intellectually, but not as fully experientially as on that occasion.

4 Hence, I was doing what Diamond (correctly in my view) claims the commentators on Coetzee's lecture misunderstood him as doing.

5 Cavell, *A Pitch of Philosophy*.

and second, some of the stories we discover might be different enough from the ones we hear closer to home to make it worth the trip. In either case, this enlarges our perspective, widens our horizons.

With all due respect, I do not think the story of Salim's mother is much like that of Jonathan's mother, except possibly from the perspective of the sons, but it would take a lengthy exposition of spirit possession in Mayotte to show why.[6] In fact, possession offers a kind of privileged communication that could be compared to the psychoanalytic encounter. Recognized spirit mediums are not psychotic, confused, or socially anomalous, and they are sometimes able to develop the sort of insight that characterizes psychoanalysis at its best.[7] Nor are mediums "spiritual" in the sense Lear's mother was described in her old age. As I noted, the word "spirit" is a poor translation for the concepts operative in Mayotte, and Euroamericans do not have an equivalent concept or metaperson.[8] It is perhaps of interest that Lear and I, from our respective areas of expertise, each accuse the other of overly hasty interpretation – promising ground for a conversation between anthropologist and psychoanalyst.

---

6 And of course, what Lear tells us about his mother is insufficient to reach an adequate description of her.

7 An interesting comparison might be between the children of mediums and those of psychoanalysts.

8 To reprise a conversation I held some thirty-five years ago with Gananath Obeyesekere comparing his psychoanalytically informed account of Sri Lankan mediums in *Medusa's Hair* (in the review essay "Ecstasy and Agony in Sri Lanka") with my cultural account in *Human Spirits*, every spirit medium is motivated by personal issues, but so are those people who do not become possessed, or who resist it, as Salim does, and so are anthropologists. But motivations play out, and are shaped, through existing cultural practices, games, or affordances, like spirit possession, anthropology, or psychoanalysis. For psychoanalytically inspired work on possession in another Muslim setting, Morocco, see Crapanzano, *The Hamadsha*; and Crapanzano, *Tuhami*. A different and complex exploration of the relationship between Islamic demons, historical trauma, psychoanalysis, and psychiatric illness in Morocco is Pandolfo, *Knot of the Soul*.

I agree that Lear or I might have faced troubles that are in some ways similar to Salim's. What I want to show is how the personal; the particular cultural vehicles, language games, and meanings; and the humanly existential all manifest in one and the same subject (actor) and acts. We cannot pull apart exactly what in Salim's condition applies to each of these domains as though they were separate layers; each affords description, and these descriptions are not mutually exclusive. As Lear says of his mother in old age, the descriptions of what happened are "equally compelling, but only in conjunction with the others."

Lear rightly brings up funerals and mourning. He says that mourning is part of our conception of "human health and well-being," more than an expression of merely being human or of human suffering, albeit elsewhere he says that *why* we mourn was a riddle for Freud.[9] A Muslim burial is held rapidly, within twenty-four hours, and several other rituals follow in relatively quick succession; in Mayotte, some months or years later, a final ceremony is held. These concern the disposal not of the body but of the soul and also close the formal obligations of the family and community to the deceased and help bring completion to the mourners. As it happens, I recently published an essay on mourning on the part of siblings whose parents had taken me as their child as well.[10] I discovered that alongside the public prayers and busy feasts that appear to ignore the individuality of the deceased and the subjectivity of the mourners, each sibling privately presented me a deeply felt account of personal witness concerning their parents' last moments or their final encounter with them. This is a cultural vehicle or language game available for healthy mourning in Mayotte, and it is one that Salim drew on in his conversation with me as well.[11]

---

9 Lear, "The Difficulty of Reality," 1206. Lear asks, "Why should mourning be considered part of what it is for humans to live well?" – a question I would begin to answer by using a word he brings up later, namely "acknowledgment."

10 Lambek, "After Death."

11 Thus he took me through the account of how he found his mother. Despite the availability of this narrative of witnessing, one is not supposed to

Lear has my utmost respect in resisting pathologizing Salim, pushing for a positive description of healthy and transient mourning rather than melancholia.[12] He is right that my description of the situation as one of tragedy could be infelicitous, stemming more from reading Cavell than from the ethnographic context. Elsewhere, Lear makes the very interesting suggestion that Freud's concept of mourning be seen as an Aristotelian virtue, a way of living well in the face of death or destruction.[13] Nevertheless, Salim himself describes his condition as one not only of grieving but *also* of pathology. His trouble "could be part of a marvellous process of acknowledging loss, separation, and connectedness," as Lear says, but that isn't how Salim described how he felt about it then or how others saw it. This was not mourning in the way I had seen it hitherto expressed in Mayotte. Of course, the forthright way in which Salim spoke to me was also new. Like Lear, I took Salim's approach as a sign more of strength than despair; I was very impressed by him, and I do imagine that he will get over his troubles, but that prediction says nothing about the source or quality of his immediate experience.[14]

I agree about malleable boundaries between self and other, and I have elsewhere applied an object relational perspective to understanding why a given medium comes to be possessed by one spirit rather than another, say a spirit who hitherto manifested in a particular parent or grandparent or who represents a desired but

talk about the deceased, and other people are not supposed to remind primary mourners about them. When I first went to Mayotte, photos of the deceased were unwelcome and *unheimlich*; later people learned the game of looking at them.

12 This exemplifies a facet of psychoanalysis at its best – that it does not make absolute discriminations between the healthy and the pathological and that it can and should be used equally well to describe positive modes of living and character formations as neurotic ones. Anthropologists have not always recognized this.

13 Lear, "Difficulty of Reality."

14 I have been unable to communicate with Salim since our original encounter and have not heard about his welfare.

rejected suitor.[15] Lear's suggestion that Salim could be defending himself from his internal mother is astute. Whether and how he might do so more productively by accepting rather than rejecting the cultural vehicle of spirit possession remains to be seen.

The trope of having a foot in more than one world is mine, not Salim's. It is *my* description of his account, not his self-description, and it may be, to make a bad pun, a left-footed one. Lear rightly corrects my assertion that this makes the situation inevitably intractable; however, it is not being in two worlds per se, but the evident pull between them *with respect to possession* that makes things difficult for Salim. What Salim needs is to find the right relation with his internal mother, in a balance that will be articulated, and perhaps resolved, by means of his relations with the spirits and hence his relative habitation in the various traditions. Moreover, the pull between autonomy and relationality – that is, the need to readjust the balance between them – is a challenge particularly salient for all members of his generational cohort in light of the rapidity of social change in Mayotte.[16]

I am not suggesting that being pulled between incommensurable elements from multiple traditions inevitably leads to psychological trouble. I see incommensurability as characteristic of, and emergent within, any and every tradition and hence that the boundary between neighbouring traditions is relative. I think that accepting incommensurability is "part of what it is for humans to live well." We must have incommensurable concepts to make sense of our lives (a point I take up further below). I fully agree that "we need to reflect more on what constitutes a life or even *a life well lived* [Lear's emphasis]." I certainly do not want to settle for "dogmatic presuppositions about what the unity of a human life consists in";[17]

---

15 Lambek, "Fantasy in Practice."
16 This is manifest in the way expectations between close kin are increasingly disappointed, giving rise to ill feeling and sometimes accusations of sorcery (Lambek, "On Sorcery").
17 That is precisely why anthropology is good to think with, though I agree with Gadamer that any view will draw from and must respond to prejudice – in the sense of "prejudgment" – of some kind.

indeed, like Austin, I am doubtful that unity need be a primary criterion for defining that life or a good life. Anthropology is in this sense itself a deeply ironic mode of living and ought to recognize irony as significant in life more generally.[18] On these points I think Lear and I concur.[19]

I also agree that our life with concepts includes using them to mislead ourselves. In talking about the inevitability of mistakes I did not consider the motivations for making them in specific instances and I thank Lear for adding that.

That was the relatively easy part of my response. Much tougher is dealing with what, borrowing a linguistic convention from Lear's own book, I call the difficulty of the difficulty of reality. I knew when I drew on Cora Diamond that I was asking for trouble, but I did not know that Lear had written an entire essay on Diamond's development of the concept.[20] I am grateful for his partial recapitulation here and accept his reading of what the difficulty of reality might mean in Diamond's sense. I acknowledge that I did not adequately support my description.

I concur that the condition of which Diamond speaks is existential. If we are predisposed to read existential difficulty in psychological terms,[21] Lear suggests I have done the reverse. But while

---

18 One reason I am sceptical of much recent criticism internal to the discipline of anthropology is that it is moralistic and unironic. Some anthropologists appear to exhibit the kind of zealotry one finds among certain Muslim or Christian reformers, recasting the practices of their predecessors or contemporaries in an overly negative light and without considering their own motivations for doing so. Too often they ignore the fact that, as David Hoy puts it, "Reflection on the partiality of past interpretations demands reflection on the partiality of the present" (*The Critical Circle*, 167). Here, I know, I sound a lot crankier and less hopeful than Lear.

19 Whether this achieves the deep form of ironic existence Lear attributes to Kierkegaard in *A Case for Irony* (discussed above) is another matter.

20 Lear, "Difficulty of Reality."

21 As Lear says about a poet ("Difficulty of Reality," 1204), "our aim is not to get to the bottom of what that poet actually thought; it is rather to explore a possibility. What if the poet were experiencing a difficulty of reality? What if he was in genuine revolt against mourning? Would the psychoanalyst then be prematurely disposed to see this as a revolt in his

Salim may not suffer as profound a disturbance of the soul as does Coetzee's fictional Elizabeth Costello, I do not think his condition is entirely psychological. I use the difficulty of reality to describe his sense of the limits to his autonomy and expectations.

With the difficulty of reality, the emphasis, says Lear, "is not on the difficulty of the experience, but rather on the experience of the difficulty." I agree that Salim's *mourning* is not a difficulty of reality, but *mourning is not the only thing at stake here*. What *is* "reality" for Salim? Reality includes the *djinn* and *sheitwan*; it includes his mother's ill-gotten gains, Salim's earlier inaction, punishment in the afterlife; and it includes the contradictory claims upon him. Perhaps at some moments this is for Salim precisely "an experience of the mind's not being able to encompass something it encounters" (to quote Lear quoting Diamond). The difficulty of reality, the astonishing inexplicability for Salim, is expressed in his marital and sexual impasse, which he understands as external to him. For him, that is not a symptom of the difficulty, it *is* part of the difficulty, the jolt. As Lear wonderfully writes, "Reality is also *being* difficult."[22] The spirits are radically unpredictable and resistant to any entreaty, and the concept of *djinn* no longer seems adequate. This is not merely a psychological (emotional) response but a cognitive and embodied one.[23]

---

mind: that is, predisposed to view the poet in exclusively psychological terms? This is how the poet might appear if he were experiencing the difficulty of reality and if he resolutely refused (what he took to be) the false comforts of mourning."

22 Lear, "Difficulty of Reality," 1200.

23 There is a sense in which Diamond's conception certainly exceeds Salim's experience and that is, insofar as Diamond's reality is something intractable, not a problem to be solved, not an aporia, but simply the way things are. "Practically speaking, difficulties may be threatening, horrifying, or overwhelming, but they do not normally present reality as too much for our concepts" (Lear, "Difficulty of Reality," 1200). In his essay on Diamond's text, Lear speaks of disorientation, of "an eruption of the issue-laden nature of our being" (1199) and "the breakdown of our normal use of concepts to contain the issues that are fundamentally our issues" (ibid). The experience is not that of loss or grief but "an experience of: the mind's inadequacy to encompass reality" (ibid). It is "a

"Diamond," writes Lear, "is trying to awaken us to an experience of inadequacy in human conceptual life itself ... It is not about
beholding that contradictions abound. It is rather about expressing an experience of the inadequacy of our concepts to encompass
the reality they are meant to encompass. The philosopher's interest
derives from our being creatures who live with and through concepts."[24] Irrespective of its appropriateness with respect to Salim, I
hope you can see why this is in tune with the broader arc of my lecture. But where I write about the inadequacy of, or mistakes with,
particular concepts, Diamond is more radical, pointing toward
those moments when the entire conceptual apparatus is revealed as
inadequate. Diamond is describing that experience; I am describing
attempts to avoid it.

Now to Lear's final provocative remarks concerning living
with the concept of anthropology. Lear asks, rather than examine Salim's life with concepts, what about anthropologists' lives
with the concept of "anthropology"? The question is deep, and
nowhere in the writing of these responses have I hesitated more.
My acknowledgment of the challenge can only be relatively shal-
low, provisional here, and unfortunately, no doubt somewhat
defensive. The first thing to say is that living with the concept of
anthropology is different from living *as* an anthropologist or, say,
with an anthropologist. This is similar to saying that for people in
Mayotte, living with the concept of spirit possession is different
from being possessed by a spirit or living with someone who is.
Yet obviously these are not unconnected. We could say that living
as is the strongest form of living *with*, the deepest commitment

---

self-conscious mode of unhappiness that recognizes of itself that it cannot
be located within the standard structure of happiness and unhappiness"
(1200). I think this is where Salim stood when I met him; *he could not make
sense of his situation.* As a parenthesis, while there is a growing amount
of anthropological literature on happiness, and a good deal on suffering,
there is less on unhappiness, or what I would call varieties of unhappiness,
that might bring together emotions like grief, melancholia, shame, or
envy, but also conditions like alienation and anomie and experiencing the
difficulty of reality.

24 Lear, "Difficulty of Reality," 1200–1.

to the concept. (There is nothing quite like the finality and visceral disruption of spirit possession to make this point.) It is in the sense of living *as* that I will continue to respond. At the same time, neither living *with* the concept or *as* an anthropologist is to be reduced to describing oneself as an anthropologist or practising anthropology.

How philosophical a response it is on Lear's part to say *attend to our own concepts*! However flawed in intention, procedure, or outcome, it has been anthropology's mission – as distinct from that of philosophers – to make available concepts that are *not* (initially) ours, especially those outside the Western tradition. Perhaps what we have to acknowledge is that doing so cannot produce justice or fairness. Nor can it solve our problems as human beings in the face of reality, a reality that is always more complex and difficult than any given concepts can handle, and a reality that includes the fact that other people think with different and interesting (but also ultimately insufficient) concepts.

It has also been an anthropological commonplace – hence a largely unexamined one – to say that grasping the concepts of others forces us to reflect on our own. Anthropology is never simply about "others" but also about "us." Anthropologists cannot produce an objective list of human values (as per Lear's remarks on the subtitle of the Tanner Lectures) and would likely recoil from attempts to do so. Yet Lear is right that anthropologists sometimes fail to fully acknowledge what anthropologist Johannes Fabian has called our coevalness with our subjects, or fail to follow philosopher Hans-Georg Gadamer's maxims that, "If we want to understand, we shall try to make [the other's] arguments even more cogent"; and "Always recognize in advance the possible correctness, even the superiority of the conversation partner's position."[25]

---

25 Fabian, *Time and the Other: How Anthropology Makes Its Object*; Gadamer, *Truth and Method*, 259–60; Gadamer, *Philosophical Apprenticeships*, 189. Of course, it could be said in defence of anthropology that we have generally done this better (less badly) than most of our contemporaries and that it has been in large part anthropology, among Western discourses, that has rendered coevalness self-evident.

Conversely, sometimes anthropologists go too far in this direction. Ethnography always exposes the ethnographer.

Living with anthropology, then, is to live in something of a suspended state of irony, recognizing that one's concepts, one's values, one's mode of living are not the only ones we could hold (or be held by) and that our commitments to them are ultimately contingent, even as we recognize the importance of making and sticking to commitments for living a meaningful and ethical life. Living with anthropology in this sense is living shadowed not only by alterity (alternatives) but by the knowledge of both the solidity (stubbornness) and the precarity of our worlds.

Living with the concept of anthropology today is also to recognize one's privilege, not only to justify adventure, to travel and study the lives of others, but to be able to sit in one's armchair and survey the vast archive of human cultural and historical diversity and experience as recorded by historians, anthropologists, and others. There is also the material privilege and ethical anxiety, if one is employed, of having adequate subsistence and sufficient political rights, while being acutely and sometimes intimately aware of those who do not. This knowledge is accompanied by scepticism concerning the ultimate value of material possessions, bourgeois personhood, concepts of freedom, progress, and the like, and knowing there are or have been other ways of living in which people might be happier or fulfilled in different ways. Living with anthropology is to be pulled between realism, politics, and romanticism.

As Lear appears to suggest, one word to describe how anthropologists live with the concept of anthropology is *uneasily*. Critique is embedded in how we pass the concept on to students and argue among ourselves. We even have a journal called *Critique of Anthropology*. As Marilyn Strathern, who has perhaps thought better than anyone about the question, puts it, "theoretical positions, in anthropology … are in fact overturned and displaced very easily – radicalisms abound."[26] Many young anthropologists

---

26 Strathern, "An Awkward Relationship," 286. My thanks to Sandra Bamford for pointing out the salience of the article.

respond to anthropology's present dilemmas by criticizing and redescribing its past. We also engage in anxious forays into other disciplines, in search of new concepts and what we too readily call "theory." Much of this is a valid response to present and past failure, but it is partly also an anxious symptom of the times and the evident insufficiency of the concept of anthropology to solve our present challenges. We rarely apply to ourselves as anthropologists the concept of "good enough," as Winnicott did to mothering.

Having made all these acknowledgments, it remains to be said that for many anthropologists, life with the concept is also necessary, even life-saving, and provides moments of exhilaration and other more continuous satisfactions that only devotion to a calling can. In sum, living with the concept of anthropology entails, ideally, the virtue and tension of irony that Lear perceives. To repeat the quotation cited in my response to Ortner, "ironic existence – considered as a human excellence – does not single-mindedly take up the cause of irony, but finds healthy and life-affirming ways of embracing the inevitable resistance to it."[27]

I would like to think that these internal matters do not preclude serious conversation with philosophers (and historians, psychoanalysts, etc.), while also recognizing that there are many kinds of anthropology and many kinds of philosophy and not all will be able to converse well with each other. Strathern famously described anthropology's relationship with feminism as *awkward*, and I expect anthropologists' relations with other disciplines are also often awkward, although likely each for their own reasons and not necessarily in the ways that she observed with respect to feminism. It might be that conversations are more valuable when they *are* (initially) awkward. This takes us back to some of the remarks at the beginning of my lecture and the observations of Ryle concerning neighbouring disciplines.[28]

---

27 Lear, *A Case for Irony*, 163. Consideration of living with the concept of anthropology continues in my response to Joel Robbins below.
28 Ryle, *Dilemmas*. See notes 3 and 14 in the initial lecture above.

Lear asks directly (but possibly rhetorically?) how well the concept of anthropology equipped me "to deal with a young man who ... asked for help." My answer is that it placed a particular (but not exclusive) description on our interaction. It helped me to listen to Salim with some understanding (differently from the understanding with which the concept of psychoanalysis might have equipped Lear to listen to Salim). It helped me to hear him then and helped me to think about a lot of other things subsequently, including what has gone into this lecture. Whether it helped Salim is a different matter, and I cannot pretend that it did (or that I did, or that I can know whether it or I did).[29] But I do not take that as a mark against anthropology.

Acknowledgment, says Lear, must include "coming to an appropriate understanding of what acknowledgment is." Such understanding could only be provisional and can only be phrased practically, not in the abstract. In Western philosophy this begins with the provocations of Socrates concerning what we do not know and continues to Wittgenstein with what we cannot put adequately into words. I acknowledge that my thoughts on the questions I have raised have not reached bottom and that my mode of explication could use some simplification. Elsewhere I have acknowledged that ethnographic fieldwork is ethically intrinsically compromised insofar as we build relations with others but always with the knowledge that we can and will leave.[30] That has not stopped me from practising it. It is rather like what people say about democracy: deeply flawed, but the least bad alternative. At least for me. Anthropology has been part of my art of living, and living does not come without continuous ethical challenge. I could even say that, like practices described by Foucault, anthropology is a discipline for ethical self-cultivation.

Acknowledgment is a matter both of deference and its insufficiency, of respecting authority and recognizing when, for what

---

29 I assume it did not harm him at the time and hope that this lecture will not either.

30 Lambek, "Ethics Out of the Ordinary." Perhaps it would be even more compromised if we stayed.

reasons, and with what motivations, we challenge authority. Acknowledgment is further a matter of recognizing the dignity of others (a point of explicit concern in Mayotte) and maintaining one's own dignity. It rubs up against but cannot be reduced to excuses.

Epistemologically, we acknowledge partiality, positionality, and the prejudicial, provisional, and precarious nature of any interpretation. Existentially, we acknowledge contingency, irony, transience, that our actions are often either premature or overdue, the difficulty of sustaining all such recognition, that we are only human, and simply, what Diamond, after Cavell, calls "exposure."[31] Such acknowledgment subjects ethnographers to the contempt of (some) scientists and the panic of positivists. My lecture, any lecture, is an act of hubris in the face of all of that. It is a matter of living as if it mattered,[32] and perhaps acknowledging that that is the best we can do.

As Lear suggests, we should acknowledge that we cannot expect the concepts drawn upon by either anthropology or philosophy to enable us to fully "face up to the difficulty of reality" or, as Geertz, in the essay cited by Robbins in his commentary, remarks, to solve either the material or the moral problems we diagnose. Maybe we should acknowledge that we "avoid the task of facing up to the difficulty of reality in the name of facing up to it" – acknowledge that abstract argument is, in Diamond's terms, deflection?[33] But that is a

---

31 Diamond, "The Difficulty of Reality," 21; Cavell, *The Claim of Reason*.
32 Lambek, "Living as if It Mattered."
33 In fact, Diamond in a footnote herself steps back from this. "That there can be such a [non-deflecting] practice [of philosophy], and that argument may have an essential role in it, is not something I would wish to deny. There are here two distinct points: philosophical argument is not in and of itself any indication that attention has been or is being deflected from the difficulty of reality, and (more positively) philosophical argument has an important role to play in bringing to attention such difficulty and in exploring its character, as well as in making clear what the limits or limitations are of philosophical argument, and indeed of other argument" ("The Difficulty of Reality," 22–3, n25).

mode of further avoidance; abstraction is recursive, like Goffman's lecture on lecturing. Maybe the most we can acknowledge is that the game we are playing is a riddle. But that should not stop us from trying to solve it, or rather, from playing as if attempting to solve it were worthwhile in itself.

Concepts and Values, Anthropology and Judgment

JOEL ROBBINS

Michael Lambek is one of the pioneering figures in the now booming anthropology of ethics. Among those who have laid the foundations for work in this area, he has done the most to focus attention on issues of practical wisdom and ethical judgment. Both theoretically and ethnographically, he has opened up for investigation the ways people sift their circumstances in moral terms as they move through the worlds they inhabit. One of the lessons Lambek has drawn from his studies in this area is how often judgments and the further actions to which they may give rise are partial, or even ironic. In keeping with this insight, his interest has been less in examining moments of decisive moral clarity or lives of sustained ascetic or pious commitment, and more in illuminating the tentative, moment-by-moment movements of judgment by which what he calls "ordinary ethics" unfolds as an aspect of all of social life. The present paper pushes his arguments in this area in a new direction by looking at how ethical judgment inheres in the way people live not just generally but with the concepts through which they understand and sometimes actively shape up the worlds in which they live. Not only is this turn to considering the ethical aspects of our life with concepts an advance in his own program, but it could not be more timely in terms of anthropological thought more generally.

It is timely because in anthropology these days, life is often thought to outrun or overwhelm the concepts by means of which people try to grasp it and render it meaningful. Many contemporary anthropologists are convinced that all sorts of pre-conceptual inner affects and intensities, on the one hand, and all sorts of both micro- and macro-structural forces that are beyond any subject's situated conscious comprehension, on the other, render the cultural concepts with which people try to bring the world under description at best the tail of the dog that really wags them and at worst fairly minor pawns in a game in which we once thought they wrote the rules. Given arguments like these, fewer and fewer scholars tend anymore to think the cultural constitution of people's worlds goes without saying, or that this is the most important thing to study when approaching their lives. It is in the face of arguments like these that Lambek's question about the ethical aspects of people's efforts to get to grips with their worlds in conceptual terms arrives as a crucial intervention in current debates. For unlike some others, he does not recommend turning our attention away from concepts. Instead, he suggests that if the world is not exhaustively or accurately given conceptually to people by the cultures they inhabit – if their lives routinely overflow or underdetermine the understandings of it offered to them by their inherited categories – then the fact that conceptualizing is always itself an act, rather than, say, a reflex, becomes all the more evident. And since, as Lambek has consistently argued across his many writings on ethics, all acts have ethical dimensions, then conceptualizing no less than any other kind of thing people do is both based on and susceptible to ethical judgment. Thus, he wagers here that perhaps focusing on the ethical aspects of living with concepts could help to rehabilitate the conceptual aspects of life more generally from the rather low place they have come to occupy in so much contemporary anthropology.

Yet even as the move to looking not just at concepts but at the ethical relation of life and concepts is an important development, it is not the only innovative part of this paper. There is a second strikingly novel part of Lambek's discussion that needs to be recognized as well if we are to fully grasp the challenge he has given us. In 1968, in an article called "Thinking as a Moral Act," Clifford Geertz pointed out that anthropological relativism is not a matter of coming to lack moral sensibilities of one's own or, worse, of finding a convenient rationale for a moral emptiness that has marked one's life all along, nor is it simply a matter of proffering some kind of logical argument about how conception and judgment work; it is rather a cultivated ability to perform a specific kind of action that is undertaken in light of "a personal subjection to a vocational ethic."[1] It is, put otherwise, a way of at least sometimes living ethically in the world. Given this ethic, Geertz continues, we have to recognize that "A professional commitment to view human affairs analytically is not in opposition to a personal commitment to view them in terms of a particular moral perspective," but is rather the cultivation of "a kind of caring [about others] resilient enough to withstand an enormous tension between moral reaction and scientific observation."[2] What Geertz is telling us by means of this argument is that anthropologists and other social scientists are making ethical judgments all the time, just like other people, but they sometimes try to hold back as much as possible the influence these judgments can have on their observational practices. The argument is not new, of course, for it goes back at least to Max Weber's classic writings on the relations of values to objectivity. But in the context of Geertz's article as a whole, which is about the moral perils of the kind of deeply embedded, open-ended, long-term fieldwork anthropologists do, which at least aspirationally involves living *with* people and not just *among* them, it takes on new valences. And these are valences that bring us back to Lambek's point that conceptual work always involves ethical judgment, now with room for Lambek's added insight that this applies to the conceptual work anthropologists do just as much as it does to that involved in any other kind of living.

In this paper, Lambek explores the gains to be had by letting go of the tension between moral judgment and observation. Toward this end, he offers his own judgments of how some other people live with concepts as a key part of his overall argument. This paper, to put this otherwise, is not just an account of how some people live with concepts, but it is also a normative argument about better and worse ways to do so. I take this turn of Lambek's argument as the provocative heart of the paper, for in making it he raises

---

1 Geertz, "Thinking as a Moral Act," 156.
2 Geertz, "Thinking as a Moral Act," 157–8.

questions the anthropology of ethics must engage if it is to wrestle with the issue of how it can inform in new ways our sense of scholarly responsibility.

The ethnographic heart of the paper is the story of a man from Mayotte named Salim. Devastated by the death of his mother, with whom he was very close, Salim is visited by the spirits who used to rise in or "possess" her. In Mayotte, spirits tend to run in families, and with the death of his mother, these spirits seek to move on to Salim. But their entreaties toward Salim cause him a good deal of distress because he does not want to have anything to do with them, since as a reformed Muslim he sees them as evil and regards any truck with them as inimical to reaching his religious goal of salvation. More than this, the presence of these spirits also torments him because it reminds him that from the point of view of his religious beliefs, his mother's embrace of these spirits may well condemn her to hellfire, and he worries that during her lifetime he might not have done enough to warn her of this danger.

As Lambek usefully acknowledges, there is a lot going on in Salim's case. He allows that this might include a good deal of unconscious processing that he did not have the opportunity to explore in the field. But what we do know, he argues, is that Salim is struggling with how to live with his concepts, particularly with those animated concepts that take the form of various kinds of spiritual metahumans that are pulling him in different directions and seemingly tearing him apart.

One thing that is crucial to the ethnographic part of the paper is the suggestion that perhaps Salim's struggles may not be necessary, for it turns out that many people in Mayotte, including Salim's mother and a man named Vita who helps Lambek understand Salim's plight, find it perfectly possible to live with both Islamic metahumans and the kind that rise in some of the people of Mayotte. At least in Vita's case, this willingness to treat both kinds of spirits as what Lambek calls incommensurable rather than opposed – that is, different from one another, but not inimical to each other nor the kinds of concept-persons between which one must choose – leads him to live a "joyous and playful" kind of life with metahumans that is clearly eluding Salim, at least at the moment Lambek encounters him.

It is important to pause to recognize a key ethnographic point here. In Salim's social world, there are at least two ways of understanding the relations between spiritual concepts tied to various kinds of spirits that, slightly inaccurately but conveniently for present purposes, we can call "local" and those belonging to Islam. One way is to recognize them as just different, "disparate" and easy to engage alongside one another in various combinations, and another, reformist Islamic one, in which local spirits have to be shunned. The first way of relating to the spirits Lambek generalizes as a "both/and" approach, while the second one, the one Salim has adopted, relates them by an either/or logic. Since both approaches exist in Salim's world, we might say that he has had to make a choice between them. I'm not sure we know Salim well enough to know if this language of choice is really a perfect fit for his case, but it is key to the logic of the argument here, for treating Salim's embrace of an either/or approach as a decision or an act, rather than, say, as an aspect of a complex way of life adopted for reasons that do not treat the relation of these sets of metahumans as the most important reason for its embrace, opens it up for judgment. And this is where this paper becomes most intriguing.

How should we judge Salim's choice? If we are going to judge him at all – and as I have already hinted in my discussion of relativism, anthropologists often would not feel compelled to – we need criteria for doing so. I have recently been doing a bit of work comparing anthropology and Christian theology as academic ways of life, and I've been struck by a key difference between them. The difference is not, as one might expect, a matter of whether both sides are equally committed to rendering judgments on their objects of study. Anthropologists more and more do judge the lives they research. As Sherry Ortner has recently noted, much of anthropology is now dark, studying situations in which people are poor, suffering, ill, and/or oppressed.[3] Those who work in these situations often want not just to describe them but also to name and judge the darkness that besets them. But it is also true that, even as

---

3   Ortner, "Dark Anthropology."

anthropologists are quicker to judge people's situations these days, we have mostly not worked out explicit criteria for doing this, so we tend to judge on the basis of our own inherited sensibilities about what good and bad lives look like. We may or may not be wrong in holding these commitments, but inasmuch as we mobilize them without much discussion of their grounding, we tend rarely to expand them or find novel, specifically anthropological ways of justifying them. This becomes clear when one turns to theology, which handles judgment in a very different way. As the eminent theologian Kathryn Tanner puts it, theologians are charged with making "normative theological judgments – judgments about what is authentically Christian."[4] In light of this commitment, it is note-worthy that one major task Christian theologians regularly engage in is arguing about the best criteria for making such judgments, be they drawn from texts, traditions, philosophical arguments, or the lived contextualizations of the faith they study. If anthropologists want to start making ethical judgments as a matter of course, if they want to collapse the tension between moral reaction and observa-tion that Geertz identified, then I think we ought likewise to begin to start making our criteria of judgment explicit and arguing about them.[5] I think Lambek has done this with courageous openness here – and that renders this a profoundly stimulating paper. But it is also an unsettling one, as it asks readers, in a way anthropolog-ical writing rarely explicitly does, to check their own judgmental criteria against the author's. I want to take up this challenge in the rest of my comment.

How does Lambek judge Salim's way of living with concepts? There are several important moments bearing on this in the paper, and I'm going to look at each one in turn. In the first, Lambek tells us how Salim's mother and Vita would judge him as having mis-takenly understood that one cannot be a pious Muslim and an "adept of spirits," for in fact they find this easy to do (32). In a foot-note (n90), Lambek points out that this is not he himself judging

---

4   Tanner, "Theology and Cultural Contest," 203.
5   Robbins, *Theology and the Anthropology of Christian Life*, 95–7.

Salim but others who are "insiders" to Mayotte. This is a perfectly grammatical move in anthropology as already constituted, so it neither raises any tricky questions nor gets us very far in the effort to surface our own judgmental criteria for discussion.

But Lambek also offers a similar judgment in his own voice. Having already told us just before invoking Salim's mother and Vita that Salim's "concepts are impoverished" because he understands Islamic and local spirits as "incompatible" (31–2), he goes on to tell us that although he recognizes that there is likely no "Archimedean" place from which to render judgment, he will describe Salim's "position as mistaken." "Writing from an appreciation of irony and life with spirits," Lambek explains, "I regret the turn Salim has taken" (38). What is the basis for this judgment?

Let me rule out one possible basis for the judgment that the paper cannot help but imply but that Lambek explicitly backs away from. This is the argument that Salim's suffering is caused by his either/or view of spirits and that his torment is the reason it is fair to say that Salim is living badly with concepts. In a footnote, Lambek states explicitly that he is not "suggesting a direct cause and effect relationship between the mistake and Salim's condition," so I think we can take this possible ground for judgment off the table (33, n95).

Having set that criterion for judgment aside, Lambek offers a general assertion, that is to say one not specific to Mayotte and any contest that might be unfolding there between reformist Islam and a more spiritually eclectic way of life, that seeing concepts as related in both/and ways is the right way to live with them, and seeing them as related in either/or ways is a mistake. Here, then, is our criterion for judgment, and it is admirably clear. I want to examine it from two distinct points of view.

One is logical and can be mentioned quickly. Surely to say that good both/and thinking that recognizes just plain difference and incommensurability between concepts is opposed to bad either/or thinking is to fail to extend to the differences between Salim's mother's and Vita's conceptual ways of life and Salim's own precisely the approach one is supposed to extend to all conceptual differences. It is an either/or judgment of condemnation wielded in service of promoting the virtues of the both/and life. Of course,

Lambek does tell us in several places that both/and thinking subsumes the either/or version, so perhaps this kind of logical argument does not hold by his reckoning. But I think when things get
this recursive and complex, we might, as Lambek very powerfully
says elsewhere in the paper, want to "choose our corrections judiciously" and perhaps not make instances of either/or thinking their
main target (50).

Moreover, even if the problems of logic and performative contradiction do not lead us to think twice about whether we can be
sure that both/and is better than either/or as a way to live with
concepts, let me suggest a second difficulty rooted more firmly in
ethnographic soil. What do we really know of Salim's ethical life?
To be sure, on one level Lambek is only judging him for a mistake
in one area of his thinking. But when we learn that Salim offers a
style of either/or thinking that characterizes "a whole movement of
reformist Islam," and also characterizes the outlook of "scientists,"
it's hard not to draw the conclusion that we are judging entire ways
of life at this point. Do we imagine that Salim and all or even a
significant number of reformist Muslims, and also that all or even
a significant number of scientists, dwell in worlds that conceptually speaking are only either/or shades of black and white, and
that, even if they did live in such entirely either/or worlds, there
is no way for them, to borrow terms Lambek uses elsewhere, to
live their lives in an ethically "meaningful, dignified, and authentic
fashion"?[6]

As phrased, I recognize that this point is a little broad, and perhaps plays to the gallery a bit by invoking core values of ethnographically seeing people's lives in the round that it is hard to argue
against. But I do think there is a real issue here. How best should
we approach differences between the lives lived by people like Salim's mother and Vita, on the one hand, and Salim himself? In constructive terms, I want to suggest an answer that I think might be
helpful. In doing so, I will momentarily leave the issue of judgment
aside; but I will come back to it in my conclusion.

---

6 Lambek, "Rheumatic Irony," 48.

The constructive move I want to make much too briefly here takes off from Lambek's quotation of Cora Diamond to the effect that there are no "evaluatively neutral" concepts we can use to bring bits of "content" under description. Anthropologists who are interested in values have known this for a long time. The point was given its fullest expression by Louis Dumont, who argued that concepts are all composed in part of values. For this reason, he liked to refer to "value-ideas" or "idea-values," and the fact that he was happy with either ordering indicates that for him they really are inseparable.[7] Putting what Dumont has in mind as simply as possible, and really just reiterating Diamond's point as I understand it, all concepts not only define some or other piece of the world, they also suggest the value it has in relation to other relevant bits of the world and the concepts that define them. So, for example, the concept "rich" does not just mean, in good structuralist binary opposition fashion, the state of not being "poor," it also means a more desirable, more valued state than that of being poor. Of course, cultural movements like, say, the one led by St Francis, can work to reverse the values that inhere in these concepts, but the concepts "rich" and "poor" remain in part constituted by values even if such movements succeed in reversing them. To adopt a term of art from philosophy, we might say that from this point of view all concepts are at least a little bit thick.

For present purposes, this is important because it means that in studying how people live with concepts we are perhaps never studying only that, we are also studying how people live with values. And when it comes to values, it is perhaps not so often the case as Lambek says it is with concepts that they are just different, incommensurable, and easy to combine. Perhaps it is more often the case with values that people feel they have to choose between them. To adopt a possibly made-up term precisely because it allows me to stay out of the well of philosophical debates about the meanings of value incommensurability and incompatibility and the like that is too deep for me at the moment, let us say that it is often the

---

7 Dumont, *Essays on Individualism*, 249 and passim.

case that in relation to one another values turn out at the very least to be "incompossible" – you just cannot put them together at one time. To take two standard average US concept-values to illustrate this point, you just can't realize at the same time the value of getting your day started and that of sleeping in. Lambek, too, tends to emphasize this incompossibility when he writes about value in this paper. Thus, he tells us that when it comes to values "we cannot hold or act on them all at once, in equal measure, or in full consistency" (12). Often, he thereby suggests, values put us in a position to make either/or choices, at least at any given moment in time, and if all concepts in part consist in values, then it might be hard completely to avoid some either/or thinking in one's life with concepts either.

But, to return to my main point, as anthropologists we know that not all lives, including lives with concept-values, look the same, and I think Lambek may well be right to suggest that lives like those of Salim's mother and Vita look different from those of Salim and maybe from those of many other reformist Muslims as well. Can our turn from concepts to concept-values help us capture this difference in a novel way? Let me work much too quickly to suggest that it can. Despite what I emphasized above, we know anthropologically that values do not always stand in either/or relations to one another. Sometimes, you can realize one value as a way to prepare yourself to realize another, often even higher value, along chains of what the anthropologist Nancy Munn calls value transformation.[8] So Lambek can realize the value of writing this lecture on the way to realizing the perhaps higher value of working out an even richer anthropological approach to ethics than he already has. Or for some people, one can leave one's family home in the morning to realize the value of working for a wage in the conviction that this wage will allow one to eventually realize the value of family life even more fully than one has before. While some values really do conflict, others really do chain up in this way.

---

8   Munn, *The Fame of Gawa.*

In thinking about the structure of relations between values, two important philosophical positions are those of value monism and value pluralism. Working much too quickly now, and taking Ronald Dworkin as my example of monism and Isaiah Berlin as the one for pluralism, we might say that monists think that all the really important values in the world, when understood rightly, chain up such that realizing lower ones always helps people possibly realize higher ones, or at least does not conflict with the effort to do so, while pluralists think that no matter how you look at it, sometimes all the important values do not chain up and people have to make either/or, or as the jargon has it, "tragic" choices between them.[9] For philosophers like Dworkin and Berlin, these are arguments about really existing, universally valid values – or at least I read them that way – and how you come down on how values are structured has a lot to do with how you think we should design our political lives. But I've wanted to borrow the distinction between pluralism and monism and treat it as an empirical matter – suggesting that societies can be ranged along a continuum between those that are more monistically organized and those that are more pluralistically organized. Of course, societies shift back and forth on this continuum over time. But the point I really want to make here is that religious movements, including those of reformist Islam and of evangelical Christianity, but also many others, tend to push for a move toward a more monistic organization. People who live in light of them often take great satisfaction, even joy, in the project of living for their highest values. But they have little interest in pursuing values that do not contribute to realizing their most important ones, and even treat doing so as wrong. I would not want to suggest that they are living badly for all that, just differently than those pluralists who, in some cases, feel free to pursue a range of different values without worrying much about which might be higher and which might be lower, or in others fret obsessively

---

9 Dworkin, *Justice for Hedgehogs*; Berlin, *The Proper Study of Mankind*; Robbins, "Monism, Pluralism."

over the tragic choices they have to make between values they hold to be equally good.

As promised, this discussion of pluralism and monism returns me to the issue of judgment. At the conclusion of his famous essay on the structural study of myth, Lévi-Strauss, whom Lambek makes such good use of in this paper, asserts that what he has been trying to prove is that everywhere and at all times human beings have "always been thinking equally well."[10] Lambek's paper takes off from a different point of view. For him, however well humans all think, they also all make conceptual mistakes, and these are, in the nature of things, ethical mistakes as well. He adds that anthropologists owe it to those they study to judge their mistakes, and it is by means of this obligation that the ethical commitments of the scholar become relevant to anthropology. I have applauded Lambek not only for being open about his desire to make the judgment of those we study part of anthropology but also for his bravery in making his criteria of judgment plain, at least those pertaining to how people live with concepts. But I have also dissented a bit from one specific criterion he has offered. I'm not convinced that a promotion of both/and thinking above either/or thinking is the way forward for anthropology, and indeed my sense is that in the history of Western thought about ethics one can find compelling schemes based broadly on both styles of thought. But I think there may also be a deeper point to be made here. Elsewhere, Lambek tells us he takes pleasure from spirit possession, and particularly from its ironic qualities – qualities that he has pioneered the way in helping anthropologists understand. Indeed, he tells us, he has "made my living" from studying spirit possession of the kind Salim's mother and Vita have practised.[11] By contrast, I have made my living studying Pentecostals who approach local spirit worlds much the way Salim does, not by denying their reality, but by rejecting them as dangerous because they are inimical to these Christians' value-projects. We might say, then, that I can't escape

---

10 Lévi-Strauss, "The Structural Study of Myth," 230.
11 Lambek, "Rheumatic Irony," 54.

knowing about the richness of lives that have a significant either/ or component, even as Lambek has cultivated enormous sympathy for both/and approaches to life. Perhaps the real lesson in this may be that if we want to develop not just an anthropology of judgment, as Lambek already so powerfully has, but also a judgmental anthropology, as he moves toward in this paper, perhaps in the first instance we should look for mistakes among the people with whom we are most engaged, to whom we are most committed, and whose lives bring us the most joy. What we are willing to judge as their mistakes, I am guessing, will give us the most useful clues as to where to look for developing criteria of judgment that could hold more widely.

Mistakes of Grammar and Anthropological Judgment
A Response to Joel Robbins

Joel Robbins exposes a knot in my argument, one that leads him to an interpretation of my lecture that is not what I thought I meant, though it may be what I (partly) said.

I began with the point that if conceptual errors are widespread in human thought, and indeed are the focus of much philosophy, anthropology has neglected them because of its justifiable mission to show, as Robbins cites Lévi-Strauss, that "everywhere and at all times human beings have 'always been thinking equally well.'"[1] Once this principle of common rationality is accepted, anthropology needs to move beyond exploring the coherence, consistency, and beauty of other cosmologies or systems of thought, and beyond the logic of practice,[2] to acknowledge that thought cannot be fully consistent and that, from certain standpoints, one can identify the same sorts of category mistakes in other societies that characterize our own thought. This point builds upon an earlier essay in which I argued, counter to certain cultural relativists, that the mind/body problem and the nature/culture problem, albeit in various guises, are universal, part of the existential condition of being human.[3] However, as Robbins rightly points out, my position is a strongly cultural one, and it is, if I can use the term, *relatively* relativist. The

---

1 Lévi-Strauss, "The Structural Study of Myth," 230.
2 Demonstrating these matters was once the means of establishing an anthropologist's reputation.
3 Lambek, "Body and Mind in Mind." This is not to discount important work like that of Descola, *Beyond Nature and Culture*, but to move to another level of abstraction.

focus is on mistakes of grammar, not on logical or empirical mistakes. Mistakes of grammar presuppose a given language game; in other words, they are internal and relative to it, not characterizable according to some absolute external measure.[4]

Robbins reads the lecture as stemming directly from my recent work on ethics, in terms I greatly appreciate. I turned to ethics because I realized that people's actions are shaped as much by virtue or judgment (in the sense of exercising one's judgment) as by power, interest, or desire, the dominant modes of explaining action in anthropology at the time. This was a reaction *against* the kind of judgmentalism that Robbins possibly reads me now as advocating! It led me further to realize that any and every act is subject to judgment in carrying it out, and it is in *this* sense, not in the sense of some intrinsic predisposition to do good, that I call the human condition an ethical one.[5] I follow Aristotle in holding that what to do, finding and following the mean, in any given circumstance is not always evident. Going beyond Aristotle, virtues might not be consistent or commensurable with one another, or sufficient to the circumstances; hence again, judgment is not self-evident or subject to algorithm, and it might not always be exercised with equanimity or agreed upon by others.

And so, in the course of preparing the lecture I was delighted to discover Cora Diamond's argument that thinking is itself moral. It is moral or ethical – terms I use interchangeably – in the sense that we exercise practical judgment in selecting and using, perhaps extending, our concepts. "Judgment" itself is a complex word (and concept) and causes confusion; I do not mean it in the legal or divine sense as something imposed top down, nor, like a prize jury, examiner, art critic, or bioethicist, conferred from outside. It is less the imposition of ethics on, or over, or after action (or in the case of ethics protocols, before action) than the expression of the ethical in and through action that concerns me: judgment is, first, immanent

---

4 Whether there is a level of universal grammar and how mistakes at that level are to be described are matters I cannot address here.

5 Lambek, *The Ethical Condition.*

to action – in the act rather than after the fact.[6] To point to grammatical mistakes is not to draw upon ostensible universal values or external criteria of judgment.

I want as well to distinguish specifically judgmental pronouncements within the broader range of judgments after the fact. This is not straightforward, since to describe particular utterances as judgmental is itself a judgment imposed on other acts of judgment, and it is perhaps itself a judgmental one. I don't know how to avoid the recursivity entailed in all this, but I do want to distinguish my judgment that Salim has made an error from being judgmental about his action. I would like to see my judgment here as neither excessively harsh or sanctimonious, nor excessively undiscriminating or undemanding (though of course Salim might receive it in one of these ways), but rather as neutral.

By following Diamond in describing thought as ethical, my description of a category mistake on the part of Salim is subject to a reading by Robbins as an ethical judgment of the imposed, judgmental, kind on my part. And I lend support to this (mistaken?) reading by making some irresponsible remarks about either/or ways of looking at the world. I need a way out of this corner, because I do not advocate a judgmental or moralistic anthropology with respect to the acts and lives of ordinary people, though I do not want an uncritical one either.[7] I do want to preserve what Geertz in his essay "Thinking as a Moral Act" calls the "tension between moral reaction and … observation."[8] Robbins's very helpful citation of Geertz's "personal subjection to a vocational ethic" provides one answer to Lear's question about living with the concept of "anthropology."

6　Grammar is similarly immanent to acts of speaking or writing.
7　With respect to the confluence of politics and social critique with ethics, see Fassin, "Troubled Waters." It is not always easy to distinguish the critical, which is in some sense necessary, from the judgmental, which is moralistic and indulgent.
8　In preparing my lecture I inexplicably ignored this essay, whose title captures such a central point. I thank Robbins both for recalling it and for summarizing it so well. "Thinking as a Moral Act" is reprinted in Geertz, *Available Light*, 21–41.

The deferral of external judgment on our subjects in favour of simply understanding them is one that explicitly marks the vocation of psychoanalysis and might apply to the vocational ethic of the anthropologist as well. A particular, and generous, conception of neutrality comes from psychoanalyst Hans Loewald, for whom, "the essence of [neutrality] is love and respect for the individual and for individual development." In a passage that ethnographers might reflect on, he says, "Scientific detachment in its genuine form, far from excluding love, is based on it ... In our best moments of dispassionate and objective analyzing we love our object, the patient, more than at any other time and are compassionate with his whole being."[9]

I do inevitably exercise judgment in the way I put things under description, but if we describe the deployment of concepts in ethical terms, so we need to extend our concept (criteria) of judgment. I describe Salim's error as grammatical, that is, as internal and relative to his language games, and *not* a matter of externally pronounced good or bad, right or wrong. Salim himself is wracked by ethical concern, and his actions are ethically fraught in that respect. I do *not* fault him for his situation, and I do *not* think it is the result of an explicit choice on his part; rather, it is the product of motivations, responses, acts, judgments, conditions, forces, and events that conjoined in a way that proved difficult for his life. I don't use the language of choice that Robbins ascribes to me.[10] I don't say we owe it to those we study to externally judge their mistakes, only to

---

9 I draw here from Stanley Stern, "My Experience of Analysis with Loewald," 1019. The first quotation is from Loewald, "The Therapeutic Action of Psychoanalysis," 229 [also found in Loewald, *The Essential Loewald*]; the second is from Loewald, "Analytic Theory and the Analytic Process," in *The Essential Loewald*, 297.

10 In Lambek, "Value and Virtue," I distinguish between choice and judgment, the former with respect to selecting between values, means, ends, or objects conceived as commensurable with one another, and the latter between those values, means, ends, or objects conceived as incommensurable. In the latter case there is no evident standard or external measure to use. I take this to be distinct from "choice," though some acts can be placed under either description.

describe them. Likewise, it is not necessarily for us to judge their judgment, only to acknowledge it *as* judgment and as *their* judgment. The critical point (on which I think Robbins and I concur) is that *we have to exercise judgment in the Aristotelian, practical sense about whether, when, and how to impose judgment in the external sense.*

In generalizing from an external perspective about either/or thinking in the abstract, I did override myself insofar as I otherwise describe judgment as practical and focused on particular circumstances.[11] Robbins is right both that, depending on context and content, an either/or position can be fine and that it is wrong to depict entire ways of life in these terms. Rather than taking an absolute position against either/or (which, as Robbins observes, would itself be a kind of either/or position of my own, hence contradictory or at best paradoxical), I was expressing the perhaps equally paradoxical position that in preferring both/and, I am simultaneously *not* selecting *between* the plural things that fall under that umbrella, things that could include an either/or position. My judgment is, in effect, to defer final judgment. (This returns to the critique made by Lear of prematurity; we can hope and expect that Salim has long since worked through his dilemma, as he evidently sought to do.) Conversely, in preferring the either/or model one risks precluding a great deal from the start, refusing to recognize or acknowledge plurality.[12]

If we are to seek and be explicit about our criteria of judgment, as Robbins suggests we should, then these are some of mine. But I am less interested in imposing external judgment on modes of living with concepts than in describing them, and especially in describing

---

11 It follows that practical judgment is not necessarily consistent in any obvious way. Over-consistency would exemplify a stance in which practical judgment is overridden.

12 The debate over gender is a case in point. As Elizabeth Anderson says, "One way gender bias reinforces sexism is through the perpetuation of categorical, dichotomous thinking which represents masculinity and femininity as 'opposites,' femininity as inferior, and nonconformity to gender norms as deviant" ("Feminist Epistemology and Philosophy of Science"). Whether to classify or not may be what Anderson calls a pragmatic decision.

the descriptions under which people put things. Life with concepts includes how, in their acts of putting things (acts, events, conditions, relations, ideas, persons) under description, people exercise judgment with respect to both concepts and persons, and conversely, how, in exercising their judgment with respect to concepts and persons, people put things under description. The mistake I am most interested in is not that of taking an either/or position per se (a mistake which, Robbins suggests, I may well have made); rather I am interested in the question of whether, in taking such a position, one mistakes incommensurable concepts for commensurable and hence possibly mutually exclusive or logically contradictory ones. However, I also suspect that making this mistake may be the only, or the easiest, way to live with certain concepts at certain times and in certain contexts. To discover a category mistake does not mean that one is able to correct it.

It is no doubt the case that where people elsewhere have taken certain concepts as incommensurable with one another we have accused them of logical error precisely insofar as we have taken these concepts (or their translation into our language) as commensurable. Here the error would be on our part. The current rejection of Cartesian dualism now fashionable has reversed all this. So now we make the mistake of praising other people for ostensibly maintaining worlds in which there are no distinctions between subjective and objective, nature and culture, and the like. I suggest closer inspection would show that such distinctions are present, but that the respective concepts are treated as incommensurable rather than commensurable and hence mutually inclusive rather than exclusive or in binary relation. Thus, for example, by certain criteria and in certain contexts, spirits and humans overlap with each other; by other criteria and in other contexts, they are taken as distinct.

If the invocation of both/and and either/or is confusing this is because it is an expression of something that may be irresolvable in human thinking, sometimes phrased as monism versus dualism. In the end, the opposition between them is itself perhaps a category mistake; hence a choice between them is not possible. As I noted in the lecture (note 137), the trick is to acknowledge and understand the prevalence of both dualism and non-dualism in human thought and practice.[13]

I am also a Gadamerian in the sense of trying, in principle, to discover, acknowledge, and possibly revise my own prejudices in the context of conversing with others and hence postponing committing to any initial moral reaction to the actions of others until I have better understood myself (as well as those others), though I confess I grow more impatient and judgmental (assured?) with age.[14] Prejudices are, in effect, the congealed consequences of prior judgment, often merely inherited. To disclose one's prejudices might also be to discover category mistakes of one's own.

That I appreciate spirit possession as I have encountered it is evident in everything I have written about it. Having committed to elucidating spirit possession and having learned from and become friends with many spirit mediums, I could hardly do otherwise. If I make my appreciation explicit, it is because possession is currently under attack, mildly but increasingly in Mayotte, and more strongly elsewhere.[15] However, I endeavour in the field to listen to everyone. I do not characterize the two positions against and for possession as respectively Islamic and local. Islam is at once global *and* local. Moreover, *both* positions are manifestations of Islam;

---

13 To shift to a different theoretical tradition and language game, one could explore these matters by means of dialectics. However, I would invoke neither subsumption nor directionality.

14 Lambek, "The Hermeneutics of Ethical Encounters." I wonder if there may be an adult life trajectory from unexamined prejudice, through openness, to standing by one's prejudices. In any case, where the tension between personal moral reaction and professional observation is too great, it is probably better to nip it in the bud. I refused to supervise a proposed doctoral project on West Bank settlers not only because I dislike and disapprove of them but because I feared that getting to know them might make me sympathetic. I think here of the very fine remark by psychoanalyst Heinz Kohut to the effect that there was no analysand whom, once he came to understand them, he could not like.

15 See for example, Adeline Masquelier, *Prayer Has Spoiled Everything*, on Niger; Stephen Selka, "Demons and Money," on Brazil; and Elizabeth McAlister, "Possessing the Land for Jesus," on Haiti.

practitioners of possession in Mayotte do not consider themselves non-Muslim or anti-Muslim. Indeed, those who accept possession might describe the reformers as un-Islamic in their prejudicial attitudes towards possession and offer historically informed critiques of the reformist position on *bid'ah* (innovation).[16]

I do not want to equate concepts with values. Moreover, my argument concerns incommensurables, whereas, as Robbins indicates, Dumont's value hierarchy is one that entails or implies commensurability.[17] I'm delighted to learn the term "incompossible," but what Robbins illustrates is also that getting your day started and sleeping in are incommensurable; we cannot put them on a common scale; it is nice to do both. I of course agree that either/or distinctions are always part of life. The problem isn't with either/or per se, but with its escalation and misuse.[18] What is described as either/or at a given moment may be redescribed as both/and over time. One day I sleep in and another I rise early. What appears either/or on Monday looks more like both/and by Sunday.[19] What I cannot do is rationally, consistently, and absolutely compare the value of comfort against that of duty; they partake of no common measure.

---

16 For extensive discussion of the relationship between Islam and spirit possession, see Lambek, *Knowledge and Practice in Mayotte*. On recent developments there, see Lambek, *Island in the Stream*.

17 Dumont is a structuralist. My argument here and, I take it, Diamond's are not structuralist.

18 Both/and and either/or are in any case Weberian idea types.

19 The way that adding a temporal dimension overcomes some of the binary distinctions in structuralism was one of the arguments of Alfonso Ortiz, *The Tewa World*. For an ethnography of Pentecostalism that takes this approach see Premawardhana, *Faith in Flux*. Drawing on William James, Premawardhana writes, "For the Makhuwa [of northern Mozambique], the alternating approach to discrete religious spheres translates into a sense that commitment to Christianity at one time and place need not preclude commitment to ancestral religion in another. The Makhuwa see no need to equate fidelity with exclusivity or sincerity with singularity. Fausto, one of my research assistants and a self-described Catholic, made the point perfectly in a discussion about Pentecostal pastors' complaints. 'It's not that we have one foot in the church and one foot in tradition,' Fausto said, 'but both feet in the church *when we're there*, and both feet on the ancestral grounds *when we're there*'" (101).

The broader point is that abstract philosophical arguments about such matters may not fit well with how people actually live the practical circumstantiality of their lives. And so, my relative dislike of rigid either/or models is not only that they oppress those who don't hold them or those who are on the wrong side but that they are also unrealistic with respect to the demands they place on their adherents and may prove a poor description of what people actually do. However, as Robbins implies, it may not be my business to say so. As already noted, I want to find a way to distinguish being judgmental from providing a full description.[20]

I cannot take up the intriguing contrast between value monism and pluralism except to say that elsewhere I have proposed distinguishing between values and meta-values, maybe even in a way a Dumontian would appreciate.[21] I agree with Robbins's point about leading fulfilling lives in monistic orders (though they can be hard on dissenters) and would draw upon Rappaport's hierarchy of sanctity to describe such orders. I admire work like Saba Mahmood's on the integrity of pious lives.[22]

In sum, I am afraid that I don't deserve Robbins's applause. I am not trying to judge those whose mistakes I describe as grammatical, and I am not advocating a judgmental anthropology.[23] I acknowledge the hermeneutic point that our position is always necessarily partial and that we need to recognize partiality, whether to try to overcome it in a given instance or simply to take it into account.

---

20 Like virtually all anthropologists, I support informed analyses of injustice, exploitation, racism, environmental destruction, and so on.

21 Lambek, "Value and Virtue." I am also saying that when values do not "chain up," as Robbins puts it, you don't need to make either/or choices but can exercise practical judgment.

22 Rappaport, *Ritual and Religion*; Mahmood, *Politics of Piety*.

23 We do of course make personal judgments and invest more or less strongly with the people we encounter in the field. Katherine Verdery, *My Life as a Spy*, offers a particularly frank (and fraught) account. And I would add that one component of my attachment to my closest interlocutors in the field was the discovery that we shared personal judgments about a number of third parties.

To be judgmental is to mistake one's own partiality and practical judgment for some kind of transcendent position.

I agree with Robbins that our judgment and values, perhaps our concepts, are influenced by the communities we study, but it may be also that our respective studies are successful and compelling insofar as what we encounter resonates with us. As a wit once said, anthropologists get the societies they deserve. However, I think that anthropology itself intrinsically holds a both/and position; a monistic perspective, say on the order of nineteenth-century evolutionism, would no longer be recognizable as anthropology.[24] Both/and thinking is the basis for the appreciation of multiple ways of life. Anthropologists rightly resist ranking them according to some value hierarchy or external measure.[25] We incorporate either/or cases like the Pentecostals by embracing them under this umbrella – appreciating them, as Robbins does – rather than putting those who don't agree with them out in the rain.

However, to convert to the position of those we study is equally to move out of anthropology. Mahmood did not become pious and adopt the veil, and Robbins has not, to the best of my knowledge, converted to Christianity or become a Pentecostalist.[26] As his generous interpretation of my work shows, Robbins, too, implicitly embraces a both/and position, albeit one that leaves ample room for the appreciation of monistic either/or alternatives.[27]

---

24 Most anthropologists turn away from evolutionary psychology and from specifically Christian or Muslim anthropologies.

25 Two exceptions: we sometimes rank societies according to population size and social scale, but these are value neutral. I am not here addressing questions of comparison, which are central to anthropology.

26 For a compelling counter-example see the film "Barbara Myerhoff: In Her Own Time," directed by Lynne Littman, 1985.

27 Joel and I have been in discussion from when as graduate students at Virginia he and Sandra Bamford edited an issue of *Anthropology and Humanism* on fieldwork in which I published an intense dialogue with a Malagasy interlocutor (Lambek, "Pinching the Crocodile's Tongue"; Emmanuel Tehindrazanarivelo, "Fieldwork: The Dance of Power") through recent debates on transcendence (Robbins, "What Is the Matter with Transcendence?") and on the good (in Henig and Strhan, eds, *Where Is the Good?*).

In sum, it is evident from the remarks of each of the commentators that the anthropological vocation entails lively ethical complexity, not least in our application of concepts and our acts of description. This is one of its lessons and one of its challenges, but also one of its attractions.

Concluding Remarks

The honour of being invited to deliver the Tanner Lecture is perhaps surpassed only by having such distinguished, intelligent, and gracious commentators, ones whose work I have long appreciated. I hope to have taken the occasion as an opportunity to extend rather than only defend my thinking. But I am also mindful of Michael Walzer's remark that argument is the very essence of collegiality. In conclusion, I recapitulate some general points from the lecture that the interlocutors did not take up directly.

The lecture tries to orchestrate at least two dialogues. One is evidently between anthropology and philosophy as I have understood and very unevenly read them. Another, perhaps more tacit, is between Geertz and Lévi-Strauss, or hermeneutics and structuralism. Here I find myself thinking through issues that were live during my education. Perhaps it is a repetition compulsion that says more about the way I think than about what I am thinking about, but these are stubborn issues, intrinsic to human being, irresolvable, and hence ones we continue to work through, or with. I was heartened when a much younger colleague told me recently how the 1970s appear to her as a period of great intellectual excitement in anthropology; so maybe it is not just my subjectivity at issue.[1]

---

1 For inspiring thought about the relationship between hermeneutics and structuralism, I owe much to my doctoral supervisor, Aram Yengoyan. It was Yengoyan who told me to read first Ricoeur, which I did with alacrity, and then Cavell, which I did not. Aram gave me a copy of *Must We Mean What We Say?*, but I found it too challenging at the time. I didn't grasp the significance of Wittgenstein until much later conversations with Jack Sidnell and Veena Das.

It is a cliché to say that the core of anthropology is the relation of unity to diversity, but I am serious in describing the universal/particular problem, like Ryle's diagnosis of the mind/body distinction, as a category mistake and serious also when I conclude that I want to tack, to paraphrase Geertz, between local detail and human experience, or, to paraphrase Cavell, between forms and life; to do so without peeling them apart as though they were discrete layers; and thereby to finesse the false opposition between the particular and the universal.

I propose that one way (among others) that anthropologists might describe what they do is the examination of how humans live with concepts.[2] One feature of our life with concepts is how we put things under description. I claim that *acts* of putting things under description are among the most common forms of social action and hence should be a central subject of ethnography, that is, one of the main things we observe, record, and think about – and indeed put under further description. Such acts ought to be made more explicit as a distinctive feature of social life. "Putting things under description" is also itself a *concept*, one that should assist anthropologists in the social analysis of particular settings (What is going on here? What is at stake? How are descriptions reached? Which out of many descriptions are relevant? How is the power to authorize descriptions wielded? What is the range of communicative forms, from ordinary talk to ritual, to bureaucracy and judicial process, to academic disciplinary practices or the Internet, by which things are put, more or less securely, under description or redescription? What are the consequences of these acts of description?). Ethnography too is a matter of putting things under description.

The concept of putting things under description applies as well to the analysis of attributions of witchcraft in Evans-Pritchard's account of the Azande as to Foucauldian accounts of power and discipline – for example, in Ian Hacking's discussion of kinds of persons.[3] It should aid us in understanding the nature of human

---

2 See also Das, *Textures of the Ordinary*; and Brandel and Motta, eds, *Living with Concepts*.

3 Evans-Pritchard, *Witchcraft, Oracles*; Hacking, *The Social Construction of What?*

existence more generally, a tool that helps us comprehend how people can talk about the same objects and events differently from one another without any of them being wrong, and how new objects come into being, in what Hacking calls historical ontology.[4] It takes social construction into account without reducing everything to the social, and it offers a circumscribed space for the relativism and complementarity of various statements and arguments. It underlies and complements Austin's account of the illocutionary and perlocutionary effects of speech, and it supports Wittgensteinian arguments concerning the ordinariness of the sorts of actions and statements that Frazer sensationalizes. It can help make us more self-conscious as to why we might call a certain act "ritual," why we might be able to describe a set of actions both as ritual and as something else, and do so without contradiction, and how we might understand what it is that what we put under the description of "ritual" does and how it works.

I argue that concepts are both incommensurable to the world they describe or account for and frequently incommensurable to each other. Mistaking incommensurable for commensurable concepts (or for contradictory ones) often takes the form of what Ryle called category mistakes, as when we mistake concepts of distinct logical types as being of the same type. Sometimes, as I suspect is the case for mind and body and for nature and culture, category mistakes may be unavoidable, symptoms, as it were, of our human condition, of our (species) being in the world. At the most abstract level this can be described as a confusion or irresolvable tension between either/or and both/and forms of relation between concepts, or the tension between monism (or non-dualism) and dualism (or pluralism).

Concepts don't have definitions so much as they have histories.[5] As concepts change over time, so what are taken to be

---

4   Anscombe, *Intention*; Hacking, *Historical Ontology*.
5   Historian Quentin Skinner argues after Nietzsche that inherited political concepts "are just *frozen conflicts*, the outcomes of ideological debate. We just get the views of the winners, so that historians always have to engage in an act of retrieval, trying to recover wider and missing structures of

incommensurable concepts in one period may become commensurable in another, or vice versa, and hence, what appears as a category mistake in one period is not so in another. However, as such changes are not instantaneous, both versions may coexist.[6] This only reinforces the point that to draw on one concept (or one use of a concept) rather than another under given circumstances entails the kind of practical reason or judgment that Aristotle applied to ethics; as Gallie noted, judgment concerning incommensurables cannot be based on a general principle. One may be unable to escape commitment to one or more of the alternatives; moreover, each act of description leaves a remainder. No single concept or system of thought or practice is able to rationally, coherently, and comprehensively capture the world. We live with incompleteness, inconsistency, and plurality – conditions that generate further thought and conversation and that make life interesting.

With respect to structuralism, the question is whether structuralists assume that we think directly by means of binary oppositions or that we impose binary classificatory schemes to order, or mediate, otherwise incommensurable concepts, that is, to practice commensuration. In note 133 of the lecture, I argued that Mary Douglas described what was untidy (hence polluting, dangerous) with respect to structures of classification already in place. While that is true, she also argued that practices of demarcation "have as their main function to impose system on an inherently untidy experience. It is only by exaggerating the difference between within and without, above and below, male and female, with and against, that a semblance of order is created."[7] It is an open question, then, which comes first, or whether, for Douglas, concepts could be as "inherently untidy" as "experience." In any case, the question is also whether, as anthropologists or philosophers or Lévi-Straussian bricoleurs, we grant more weight to tidy classifications or

---

debate" (in Lévy and Tricoire, interview with Quentin Skinner, "Concepts Only Have Histories," accessed 21 March 2020: https://www.espacestemps .net/articles/quentin-skinner/).

6 Koselleck, *Futures Past*, the contemporaneity of the non-contemporaneous.
7 Douglas, *Purity and Danger*, 13.

untidy concepts, or examine how both play a part in our lives and thought. I'm suggesting that category mistakes, a kind of concealed untidiness, are one unanticipated outcome of commensuration, or one form that commensuration takes.

Living with concepts, I have suggested, can be compared to living with persons. We hold commitments to each and they to us, being more or less reliable and consistent and more or less in harmony or conflict with other persons or other concepts, respectively. Concepts and persons are also closely interdependent; persons and interpersonal relations are premised on concepts of kinship, hospitality, and the like. Conversely, our relations with concepts cannot be described in purely abstract terms, as grammatical alone, but also in terms of personal attachments, implicit prejudices and explicit commitments, affects and effects. If some applications of concepts contribute positively to human experience, some concepts serving perhaps as our companions, others are harmful or hurtful in particular circumstances; concepts *matter* to people. As Wittgenstein knew well, and as thinkers like Das, Diamond, and Lear have drawn from his work, the grammatical is also personal.

I argue that concepts and persons are inextricably conjoined in the figures of metahumans (metapersons), as these are reproduced conceptually and personally in intellectual (theological) arguments, ritual acts, and subjective experience.[8] Deities become more or less personalized over historical time, but also in phenomenological or subjective time, from moment to moment or circumstance to circumstance, as in Robert Orsi's descriptions of coming into presence.[9] Metahumans afford personal relations with concepts and conceptual relations with persons. I trust that making this plastic double nature of metahumans explicit will help in the ongoing anthropological project of at once both taking our interlocutors seriously and de-essentializing constructs like "god/s," "spirit/s," "demons," "religion," and so on, that constitute our comparative

---

8 See the remarkable argument by Kenneth Burke, *Rhetoric of Religion*, in which language and God stand in analogical and mutually illuminating relation to one another. My thanks to Paul Antze for directing me to it.

9 Orsi, *History and Presence*.

toolkit. This might also shift the way we think about kinship or any form of person address or social relationship. In describing relations with and among metahumans, a relatively untapped resource has been the concept of grammar, in both the straightforward linguistic sense (the work of parts of speech in distinct languages) and in the Wittgensteinian sense, and the ways in which these inform each other. These projects, like so many of the arguments raised but not fully addressed in the course of this lecture, remain to be developed.[10]

In sum, faced with the incommensurable concepts and metapersons that constitute our forms of life, we exercise practical judgment as we draw on them, whether within a given language game or in distinguishing between games (themselves incommensurable with one another). At times we reach an impasse, and sometimes we make mistakes. We should not suppose the existence of human worlds whose inhabitants are not subject to dilemma, debate, uncertainty, error, and ethical aporia on the same order as the rest of us. To end full circle with Lévi-Strauss, "All problems pertaining to humankind are ultimately problems for humankind." We can approach the human condition only by means of conceptual distinctions that human beings cannot overcome, and we should acknowledge that this is what we do.

---

10 See, for example, Quincy Amoah, "Ejok! Experience, Language, and Aesthetico-Moral Expression in Karamoja," and his forthcoming work on Nilotic grammar and thought.

References

Ahmed, Shahab. *What Is Islam? The Importance of Being Islamic.* Princeton, NJ: Princeton University Press, 2015.

Amoah, Quincy J. "Ejok! Experience, Language, and Aesthetico-Moral Expression in Karamoja." PhD diss., Department of Anthropology, Princeton University, 2020.

Anderson, Elizabeth. *Value in Ethics and Economics.* Cambridge, MA: Harvard University Press, 1993.

– "Feminist Epistemology and Philosophy of Science." In *The Stanford Encyclopedia of Philosophy*, edited by Edward N. Zalta, Spring ed., 2020. https://plato.stanford.edu/archives/spr2020/entries/feminism-epistemology/.

Anscombe, G.E.M. *Intention.* Ithaca, NY: Cornell University Press, 1963.

Appiah, Anthony. *Experiments in Ethics.* Cambridge, MA: Harvard University Press, 2008.

Aquinas, St Thomas. *Summa Theologiae*, first part, 32–8. Online ed., © Kevin Knight. np: New Advent, 2017.

Arendt, Hannah. *The Human Condition.* 2nd ed. Chicago: University of Chicago Press, 1958.

Austin, J.L. *How to Do Things with Words.* Oxford: Oxford University Press, 1965.

– "A Plea for Excuses." In his *Philosophical Papers*, 175–204. Oxford: Oxford University Press, 1970.

Bakhtin, Mikhail. *The Dialogic Imagination: Four Essays.* Edited by Michael Holquist and translated by Caryl Emerson and Michael Holquist. Austin: University of Texas Press, 1981.

Barker, Joshua, Erik Harms, and Johan Lindquist, eds. *Figures of Southeast Asian Modernity.* Honolulu: University of Hawai'i Press, 2013.

Bateson, Gregory. *Steps to an Ecology of Mind*. Chicago: University of Chicago Press, 1972.

Berger, Peter, and Thomas Luckmann. *The Social Construction of Reality*. London: Penguin, 1966.

Berlin, Isaiah. *The Proper Study of Mankind: An Anthology of Essays*. New York: Farrar, Straus and Giroux, 1998.

Bernstein, Richard. *Beyond Objectivism and Relativism: Science, Hermeneutics, and Praxis*. Philadelphia: University of Pennsylvania Press, 1983.

Bloch, Maurice. "Ritual and Deference." In *Essays on Cultural Transmission*, edited by Maurice Bloch, 123–37. Oxford: Berg, 2005.

Boddy, Janice. *Wombs and Alien Spirits*. Madison: University of Wisconsin Press, 1989.

Bourdieu, Pierre. *Distinction: A Social Critique of the Judgment of Taste*. Translated by Richard Nice. Oxford: Routledge, 1984.

– *The Logic of Practice*. Translated by Richard Nice. Cambridge: Polity, 1990.

Brague, Rémi. "God." In *The Dictionary of Untranslatables: A Philosophical Lexicon*, edited by Barbara Cassin. Princeton, NJ: Princeton University Press, 2014.

Brandel, Andrew, and Marco Motta, eds. *Living with Concepts: Anthropology in the Grip of Reality*. New York: Fordham University Press, 2021.

Breuer, Josef, and Sigmund Freud. *Studies on Hysteria*. London: Hogarth Press, 1955.

Burke, Kenneth. *A Grammar of Motives*. Berkeley: University of California Press, 1945.

– *The Rhetoric of Religion: Studies in Logology*. Boston: Beacon, 1961.

Canfield, Jack. "The Living Language: Wittgenstein and the Empirical Study of Communication." *Language Sciences* 15, no. 3 (1993): 165–93.

Cassin, Barbara, ed. *The Dictionary of Untranslatables: A Philosophical Lexicon*. English "translation" edited by Emily Apter, Jacques Lezra, and Michael Wood. Princeton, NJ: Princeton University Press, 2014 [2004].

Cavell, Stanley. "The Availability of Wittgenstein's Later Philosophy." In his *Must We Mean What We Say?*, 44–72. Cambridge: Cambridge University Press, 1976.

– "The Avoidance of Love." In *Must We Mean What We Say?*, 267–353. Cambridge: Cambridge University Press, 1976.

– *The Claim of Reason*. Oxford: Clarendon Press, 1979.

– *A Pitch of Philosophy*. Cambridge, MA: Harvard University Press, 1996.

Coetzee, J.M. *The Lives of Animals*. Tanner Lectures. Edited by Amy Gutt-mann. Princeton, NJ: Princeton University Press, 1999.

Crapanzano, Vincent. *The Hamadsha: A Study in Moroccan Ethnopsychiatry*. Berkeley: University of California Press, 1981.

– *Tuhami: Portrait of a Moroccan*. Chicago: University of Chicago Press, 1985.

Critchley, Simon. "Cavell's 'Romanticism' and Cavell's Romanticism." In *Contending with Stanley Cavell*, edited by Russell Goodman, 37–54. Oxford: Oxford University Press, 2005.

Das, Veena. *Life and Words: Violence and the Descent into the Ordinary*. Berkeley: University of California Press, 2007.

– "What Does Ordinary Ethics Look Like?" In *Four Lectures on Ethics: Anthropological Perspectives*, by Michael Lambek, Veena Das, Didier Fassin, and Webb Keane, 52–125. Chicago: Hau Books, 2015.

– "Resemblance and Resonance: Two Modes of Relating." Paper presented at the annual meeting of the American Ethnological Society, Philadelphia, March 2018.

– *Textures of the Ordinary: Doing Anthropology after Wittgenstein*. New York: Fordham University Press, 2020.

– "The Life of Concepts: In the Vicinity of Dying." In *Textures of the Ordinary: Doing Anthropology after Wittgenstein*, 307–32. New York: Fordham University Press, 2020.

Das, Veena, Michael Jackson, Arthur Kleinman, and Bhrigupati Singh, eds. *The Ground Between: Anthropologists Engage Philosophy*. Durham, NC: Duke University Press.

Daston, Lorraine. "The Morality of Natural Orders: The 'Power of Medea' and 'Nature's Customs Versus Nature's Laws.'" The Tanner Lectures on Human Values, delivered at Harvard University, Cambridge, MA, 2002.

Deleuze, Gilles, and Félix Guattari. *What Is Philosophy?* New York: Columbia University Press, 1996.

Descola, Philippe. *Beyond Nature and Culture*. Translated by Janet Lloyd. Chicago: University of Chicago Press, 2013.

– "Presence, Attachment, Origin: Ontologies of 'Incarnates.'" In *A Companion to the Anthropology of Religion*, edited by Janice Boddy and Michael Lambek, 35–49. Malden, MA: Wiley-Blackwell, 2013.

Detienne, Marcel. *Comparative Anthropology of Ancient Greece*. Cambridge, MA: Harvard University Press, Center for Hellenic Studies, 2009.

Dewey, John. "The Need for a Recovery of Philosophy (1917)." In *The Essential Dewey*, vol. 1, edited by Larry Hickman and Thomas Alexander. Bloomington: Indiana University Press, 1998.

Diamond, Cora. "Losing Your Concepts." *Ethics* 98, no. 2 (1988): 255–77.

– "The Importance of Being Human." *Royal Institute of Philosophy Supplement* 29 (1991): 35–62.

– "'We Are Perpetually Moralists': Iris Murdoch, Fact and Value." In *Iris Murdoch and the Search for Human Goodness*, edited by Maria Antonaccio and William Schweiker, 79–109. Chicago: University of Chicago Press, 1996.

– "The Difficulty of Reality and the Difficulty of Philosophy." *Partial Answers: Journal of Literature and the History of Ideas* 1 (2003): 1–26.

– "Criticising from 'Outside.'" *Philosophical Investigations* 26, no. 2 (2013): 114–32.

– "Thoughts about Irony and Identity." In Jonathan Lear, *A Case for Irony*, chapter 7, 128–53. Cambridge, MA: Harvard University Press, 2014.

– "Von Wright on Wittgenstein in Relation to His Times." 2016. http://www.helsinki.fi/wwa/von_Wright_Lecture.html.

Douglas, Mary. *Purity and Danger*. London: Penguin, 1966.

Dumont, Louis. *Essays on Individualism: Modern Ideology in Anthropological Perspective*. Chicago: University of Chicago Press, 1986.

Dworkin, Ronald. *Justice for Hedgehogs*. Cambridge, MA: Harvard University Press, 2011.

Evans-Pritchard, E.E. *Witchcraft, Oracles and Magic among the Azande*. Oxford: Clarendon Press, 1937.

– *The Nuer*. Oxford: Clarendon Press, 1940.

Fabian, Johannes. *Time and the Other: How Anthropology Makes Its Object*. New York: Columbia University Press, 1983.

Farmer, Paul. "Never Again? Reflections on Human Values and Human Rights." In *The Tanner Lectures on Human Values*, edited by G.B. Peterson, vol. 26, 137–88. Salt Lake City: University of Utah Press, 2006.

Fassin, Didier. "Troubled Waters: At the Confluence of Ethics and Politics." In *Four Lectures on Ethics: Anthropological Perspectives*, by Michael Lambek, Veena Das, Didier Fassin, and Webb Keane, 175–210. Chicago: Hau Books, 2015.

Foot, Philippa. "Moral Realism and Moral Dilemma." In her *Moral Dilemmas*, 37–58. Oxford: Clarendon Press, 2002.

Frankfurt, Harry. *Taking Ourselves Seriously and Getting It Right: The Tanner Lectures*. Edited by Debra Satz. Stanford, CA: Stanford University Press, 2006.

Gadamer, Hans-Georg. *Philosophical Apprenticeships*. Translated by Robert R. Sullivan. Cambridge, MA: MIT Press, 1985.

– *Truth and Method*. New York: Crossroad, 1985 [1960].

Gallie, W.B. "Essentially Contested Concepts." *Proceedings of the Aristotelian Society, New Series* 56 (1955–6): 167–98.

Geertz, Clifford. "Deep Play: Notes on the Balinese Cockfight." In *The Interpretation of Cultures*, 412–53. New York: Basic Books, 1973.

– "Thick Description." In *The Interpretation of Cultures*, 3–30. New York: Basic Books, 1973.

– "The Growth of Culture and the Evolution of Mind." In *The Interpretation of Cultures*, 55–83. New York: Basic Books, 1973 [1962].

– "The Impact of the Concept of Culture on the Concept of Man." In *The Interpretation of Cultures*, 33–54. New York: Basic Books, 1973 [1966].

– "Blurred Genres: The Refiguration of Social Thought." In *Local Knowledge: Further Essays in Interpretive Anthropology*, 19–35. New York: Basic Books, 1983.

– "From the Native's Point of View." In *Local Knowledge*, 55–70. New York: Basic Books, 1983.

– "The Uses of Diversity." The Tanner Lecture, University of Michigan, Ann Arbor, 1985.

– *Available Light: Anthropological Reflections on Philosophical Topics*. Princeton, NJ: Princeton University Press, 2000.

– "Passage and Accident: A Life of Learning." In *Available Light*, 3–20. Princeton, NJ: Princeton University Press, 2000.

– "Thinking as a Moral Act: Ethical Dimensions of Anthropological Fieldwork in the new States." In *Available Light*, 21–41. Princeton, NJ: Princeton University Press, 2000.

Gibbard, Allan. *Wise Choices, Apt Feelings*. Cambridge, MA: Harvard University Press, 1990.

Goethe, Johann Wolfgang von. *Faust: Part I*. Cambridge, MA: The Harvard Classics, 1909–14 [1808].

Goffman, Erving. *The Presentation of Self in Everyday Life*. New York: Doubleday, 1956.

– "Footing." In *Forms of Talk*, edited by Erving Goffman, 124–59. Philadelphia: University of Pennsylvania Press, 1981.

Graeber, David. *Toward an Anthropological Theory of Value*. New York: Palgrave Macmillan, 2001.

Hacking, Ian. *Social Construction of What?* Cambridge, MA: Harvard University Press, 1999.

– *Historical Ontology*. Cambridge, MA: Harvard University Press, 2002.

Haeri, Niloofar. *Say What Your Longing Heart Desires: Women, Prayer, and Poetry in Iran*. Stanford, CA: Stanford University Press, 2020.

Hartman, David. "Judaism as an Interpretive Tradition." In his *A Heart of Many Rooms*, 3–36. Woodstock, VT: Jewish Lights Publishing, 1999.

– *The God Who Hates Lies: Confronting and Rethinking Jewish Tradition*. Woodstock, VT: Jewish Lights Publishing, 2011.

Hartman, Donniel. *Putting God Second: How to Save Religion from Itself*. Boston: Beacon, 2016.

Henig, David, and Anna Strhan, eds. *Where Is the Good?* Oxford: Berghahn, forthcoming.

Hollis, Martin, and Steven Lukes, eds. *Rationality and Relativism*. Cambridge, MA: MIT Press, 1982.

Hoy, David. *The Critical Circle*. Berkeley: University of California Press, 1978.

Humphrey, Caroline. "Exemplars and Rules: Aspects of the Discourse of Moralities in Mongolia." In *The Ethnography of Moralities*, edited by Signe Howell. London: Routledge, 1997.

Ingold, Tim. "Editorial." *Man, New Series* 27, no. 4 (1992): 693–6.

Jackson, Michael. *Minima Ethnographica: Intersubjectivity and the Anthropological Project*. Chicago: University of Chicago Press, 1998.

– *Existential Anthropology: Events, Exigencies, and Effects*. New York: Berghahn, 2005.

James, William. *The Meaning of Truth*. New York: Longman Green, 1909.

Johnson, Paul Christopher. "Toward an Atlantic Genealogy of Spirit Possession." In *Spirited Things: The Work of "Possession" in Afro-Atlantic Religions*, edited by Paul Christopher Johnson, 23–46. Chicago: University of Chicago Press, 2014.

Jorgensen, Dan. "What's in a Name: The Meaning of Meaningless in Telefolmin." *Ethos* 8 (1980): 349–66.

Keane, Webb. *Ethical Life: Its Natural and Social Histories*. Princeton, NJ: Princeton University Press, 2016.

Kenny, Sir Anthony. "Anthropomorphism vs Humanism." The Georg Henrik von Wright Lecture, Helsinki, 2014.

Koselleck, Reinhart. *Futures Past: On the Semantics of Historical Time.* Translated by Keith Tribe. New York: Columbia University Press, 2004.

Kresse, Kai. *Philosophizing in Mombasa.* Oxford: Oxford University Press, 2007.

Kuhn, Thomas. *The Structure of Scientific Revolutions.* 3rd ed. Chicago: University of Chicago Press, 1996 [1962].

Lambek, Joachim. "Foundations of Mathematics." Accessed 30 March 2018. https://www.britannica.com/science/foundations-of-mathematics/.

Lambek, Joachim, and Philip Scott. "Reflections on the Categorical Foundations of Mathematics." *Foundational Theories of Classical and Constructive Mathematics: The Western Ontario Series in Philosophy of Science 76* (2011): 171–86. Special issue edited by G. Sommaruga.

Lambek, Michael. *Human Spirits: A Cultural Account of Trance in Mayotte.* Cambridge: Cambridge University Press, 1981.

– "Ecstasy and Agony in Sri Lanka." Review article, *Comparative Studies in Society and History* 27, no. 2 (1985): 291–303.

– *Knowledge and Practice in Mayotte: Local Discourses of Islam, Sorcery, and Spirit Possession.* Toronto: University of Toronto Press, 1993.

– "Pinching the Crocodile's Tongue: Affinity and the Anxieties of Influence in Fieldwork." *Anthropology and Humanism* 22, no. 1 (1997): 31–53. Special issue edited by Sandra Bamford and Joel Robbins.

– "Body and Mind in Mind, Body and Mind in Body: Some Anthropological Interventions in a Long Conversation." In *Bodies and Persons: Comparative Perspectives from Africa and Melanesia,* edited by M. Lambek and Andrew Strathern, 103–23. Cambridge: Cambridge University Press, 1998. Reprinted in Henrietta Moore and Todd Sanders, eds, *Anthropology in Theory: Issues in Epistemology.* Boston: Wiley-Blackwell, 2014.

– "Fantasy in Practice: Projection and Introjection, or the Witch and the Spirit-Medium." In *Beyond Rationalism: Rethinking Magic, Witchcraft and Sorcery,* edited by Bruce Kapferer, 198–214. New York: Berghahn, 2002. Co-published in *Social Analysis* 46, no. 3: 198–214.

– *The Weight of the Past: Living with History in Mahajanga, Madagascar.* New York: Palgrave Macmillan, 2002.

– "Rheumatic Irony: Questions of Agency and Self-Deception as Refracted through the Art of Living with Spirits." In *Illness and Irony,* edited by M. Lambek and Paul Antze, 40–59. New York: Berghahn, 2003.

- "Provincializing God? Provocations from an Anthropology of Religion." In *Religion: Beyond a Concept*, edited by Hent de Vries, 120–38. New York: Fordham University Press, 2008.
- "Afterword: How the Figure Figures." In *Figuring the Transforming City*, edited by Mieke de Gelder, Sheri Gibbings, and Joshua Barker. Special issue of *City & Society* 25, no. 2 (2013): 271–7.
- "The Continuous and Discontinuous Person: Two Dimensions of Ethical Life." *Journal of the Royal Anthropological Institute* 19 (2013): 837–58.
- "What Is 'Religion' for Anthropology?" In *Companion to the Anthropology of Religion*, edited by Janice Boddy and Michael Lambek, 1–32. Boston: Wiley-Blackwell, 2013.
- "Afterword: Recognizing and Misrecognizing Spirit Possession." In *Spirited Things: The Work of "Possession" in Afro-Atlantic Religions*, edited by Paul Christopher Johnson, 257–76. Chicago: University of Chicago Press, 2014.
- "The Interpretation of Lives or Life as Interpretation: Cohabiting with Spirits in the Malagasy World." *American Ethnologist* 41, no. 3 (2014): 491–503.
- *The Ethical Condition: Essays on Action, Person, and Value*. Chicago: University of Chicago Press, 2015.
- "The Ethical Condition." In *The Ethical Condition*, 1–39. Chicago: University of Chicago Press, 2015.
- "Ethics Out of the Ordinary." In *The Ethical Condition*, 267–81. Chicago: University of Chicago Press, 2015.
- "The Hermeneutics of Ethical Encounters." In *Speaking Ethically across Borders*, edited by Jonathan Mair and Nicholas Evans. Special section of *Hau* 5, no. 2 (2015): 227–50.
- "Living as if It Mattered." In *Four Lectures on Ethics*, by Michael Lambek, Veena Das, Didier Fassin, and Webb Keane, 5–51. Chicago: Hau Books, 2015.
- "Value and Virtue." In *The Ethical Condition*, 214–41. Chicago: University of Chicago Press, 2015.
- "After Death: Event, Narrative, Feeling." In *A Companion to the Anthropology of Death*, edited by Antonius Robben, 87–101. Boston: Wiley-Blackwell, 2018.
- *Island in the Stream: An Ethnographic History of Mayotte*. Toronto: University of Toronto Press, 2018.
- "Remarks on Wittgenstein's Remarks on Frazer." In *The Mythology in Our Language: Remarks on Frazer's Golden Bough*, edited by Stephan Palmié and Giovanni da Col. Chicago: Hau Books, 2020.

– "On Sorcery: Life with the Concept." In *Living with Concepts: Anthropology in the Grip of Reality*, edited by Andrew Brandel and Marco Motta. New York: Fordham University Press, 2021.

Latour, Bruno. *We Have Never Been Modern*. Cambridge, MA: Harvard University Press, 1991.

Leach, E.R., ed. *Dialectic in Practical Religion*. Cambridge: Cambridge University Press, 1968.

Lear, Jonathan. *Therapeutic Action: An Earnest Plea for Irony*. New York: Other Press, 2003.

– *Radical Hope: Ethics in the Face of Cultural Devastation*. Cambridge, MA: Harvard University Press, 2008.

– *A Case for Irony*. The Tanner Lectures on Human Values. Cambridge, MA: Harvard University Press, 2014 [2011].

– "The Difficulty of Reality and a Revolt against Mourning." *European Journal of Philosophy* (2018): 1–12.

Lévi-Strauss, Claude. "The Structural Study of Myth." In *Structural Anthropology I*, translated by Claire Jacobson and Brooke Grundfest Schoepf, 206–31. New York: Basic Books, 1963.

– *The Savage Mind (La Pensée Sauvage)*. Chicago: University of Chicago Press, 1966. Retranslated by Jeffrey Mehlman and John Leavitt as *Wild Thought*. Chicago: University of Chicago Press, 2021.

– *The Raw and the Cooked: Mythologiques*. Translated by John Weightman and Doreen Weightman, vol. 1. Chicago: University of Chicago Press, 1983 [1964].

– "Anthropology and the 'Truth Sciences.'" Edited by Andrew Brandel and Sidney Mintz. *Hau: Journal of Ethnographic Theory* 3, no. 1 (2013 [1978]): 241–8.

Lévy, Jacques, and Emmanuelle Tricoire. "Concepts Only Have Histories." Interview with Quentin Skinner. Accessed 21 March 2020. https://www.espacestemps.net/articles/quentin-skinner/.

Lienhardt, Godfrey. *Divinity and Experience*. Oxford: Oxford University Press, 1961.

Loewald, Hans W. "On Internalization." "Ego-Organization and Defense." "Primary Process, Secondary Process and Language." "The Therapeutic Action of Psychoanalysis." "Internalization, Separation, Mourning and the Superego." In *The Essential Loewald*. Haggerstown, MD: University Publishing Group, 2000.

MacDonald, D.B., H. Massé, P.N. Boratav, K.A. Nizami, and P. Voorhoeve. "Djinn." In *Encyclopaedia of Islam*, edited by P. Bearman, Th.

Bianquis, C.E. Bosworth, E. van Donzel, and W.P. Heinrichs. 2nd ed. Accessed 7 May 2018. https://referenceworks.brillonline.com/entries /encyclopaedia-of-islam-2/*-COM_0191.

MacIntyre, Alasdair. *After Virtue*. South Bend, IN: University of Notre Dame Press, 1981.

Macpherson, C.B. *Democratic Theory: Essays in Retrieval*. Oxford: Clarendon Press, 1973.

Mahmood, Saba. *Politics of Piety: The Islamic Revival and the Feminist Subject*. Princeton, NJ: Princeton University Press, 2005.

Malaby, Thomas. *Gambling Life: Dealing in Contingency in a Greek City*. Champaign, IL: University of Illinois Press, 2003.

Margolis, Eric, and Stephen Laurence. "Concepts." In *The Stanford Encyclopedia of Philosophy*, edited by Edward N. Zalta, 2014. https://plato.stanford.edu/archives/spr2014/entries/concepts/.

Masquelier, Adeline. *Prayer Has Spoiled Everything: Possession, Power, and Identity in an Islamic Town of Niger*. Durham, NC: Duke University Press, 2001.

Mattingly, Cheryl. *Moral Laboratories: Family Peril and the Struggle for a Good Life*. Berkeley: University of California Press, 2014.

Mattingly, Cheryl, and Thomas Schwarz Wentzer. "Toward a New Humanism: An Approach from Philosophical Anthropology." *Hau* 8 (2018): 144–57.

McAlister, Elizabeth. "Possessing the Land for Jesus." In *Spirited Things: The Work of "Possession" in Afro-Atlantic Religions*, edited by Paul Christopher Johnson, 177–205. Chicago: University of Chicago Press, 2014.

Merton, Robert K. "A Life of Learning." ACLS Occasional Paper 25, American Council of Learned Societies, New York, 1994.

Monk, Ray. *Ludwig Wittgenstein: The Duty of Genius*. New York: The Free Press, 1990.

Moody-Adams, Michele. *Fieldwork in Familiar Places: Morality, Culture, and Philosophy*. Cambridge, MA: Harvard University Press, 2002.

Moore, Henrietta, and Todd Sanders, eds. *Anthropology in Theory: Issues in Epistemology*. Boston: Wiley-Blackwell, 2014.

Mulhall, Stephen. *The Great Riddle: Wittgenstein and Nonsense, Theology and Philosophy*. Oxford: Oxford University Press, 2015.

Munn, Nancy M. *The Fame of Gawa: A Symbolic Study of Value Transformation in a Massim (Papua New Guinea) Society*. New York: Cambridge University Press, 1986.

Murdoch, Iris. "Vision and Choice in Morality." *Proceedings of the Aristotelian Society* 30, suppl. (1956): 42–3.

Myerhoff, Barbara. "Barbara Myerhoff: In Her Own Time." Film directed by Lynne Littman, 1985.

Narboux, Jean-Philippe. "Actions and Their Elaboration." In *Must We Mean What We Say at Fifty*, edited by Greg Chase, Juliet Floyd, and Sandra Laugier. Cambridge: Cambridge University Press, in press.

Nehamas, Alexander. *The Art of Living: Socratic Reflections from Plato to Foucault*. Berkeley: University of California Press, 1998.

Nietzsche, Friedrich. "On Truth and Lying in an Nonmoral Sense." In *Truth: Engagements across Philosophical Traditions*, edited by José Medina and David Wood, 14–25. Malden, MA: Wiley-Blackwell, 2008. [1873].

Nuttall, Mark. *Arctic Homeland: Kinship, Community and Development in Northwest Greenland*. Toronto: University of Toronto Press, 1992.

– "Arctic Weather Words." *Anthropology News* 59, no. 2 (2018): 6–10.

Obeyesekere, Gananath. *Medusa's Hair: An Essay on Personal Symbols and Religious Experience*. Chicago: University of Chicago Press, 1981.

Orsi, Robert. *Between Heaven and Earth: The Religious Worlds People Make and the Scholars Who Study Them*. Princeton, NJ: Princeton University Press, 2005.

– *History and Presence*. Cambridge, MA: Harvard University Press, 2016.

Ortiz, Alfonso. *The Tewa World: Space, Time, Being and Becoming in a Pueblo Society*. Chicago: University of Chicago Press, 1969.

Ortner, Sherry B. "On Key Symbols." *American Anthropologist* 75, no. 5 (1973): 1338–46.

– *Sherpas through Their Rituals*. Cambridge: Cambridge University Press, 1978.

– *Making Gender: The Politics and Erotics of Culture*. Boston: Beacon Press, 1996.

– *Life and Death on Mt Everest*. Princeton, NJ: Princeton University Press, 1999.

– *Anthropology and Social Theory: Culture, Power, and the Acting Subject*. Durham, NC: Duke University Press Books, 2006.

– "Power and Projects: Reflections on Agency." In *Anthropology and Social Theory*, 129–54. Durham, NC: Duke University Press Books, 2006.

– "Dark Anthropology and Its Others: Theory since the Eighties." *Hau: Journal of Ethnographic Theory* 6, no. 1 (2016): 47–73.

Otto, Rudolf. *The Idea of the Holy*. Oxford: Oxford University Press, 1923.

Otto, Ton, and Rane Willerslev, eds. "Value as Theory." *Hau* 3 (2013), special issue 3.1 and 3.2.

Palmié, Stephan, and Giovanni da Col, eds. *The Mythology in Our Language: Remarks on Frazer's Golden Bough*. Chicago: Hau Books, 2020.

Pandolfo, Stefania. *Knot of the Soul: Madness, Psychoanalysis, Islam*. Chicago: University of Chicago Press, 2017.

Parker, Robert. *On Greek Religion*. Ithaca, NY: Cornell University Press, 2011.

Pope, Alexander. *An Essay on Man*. London: Lawton Gilliver, 1734.

Pouillon, Jean. "Remarks on the Verb 'to Believe.'" In *Between Belief and Transgression*, edited by Michel Izard and Pierre Smith. Chicago: University of Chicago Press, 1982. Reprinted in M. Lambek, ed., *A Reader in the Anthropology of Religion*. 2nd ed. Malden, MA: Blackwell, 2008.

Premawardhana, Devaka. *Faith in Flux: Pentecostalism and Mobility in Rural Mozambique*. Philadelphia: University of Pennsylvania Press, 2018.

Radin, Paul. *Primitive Man as Philosopher*. New York: New York Review Books Classics, 2017 [1927].

Rappaport, Roy. *Ritual and Religion in the Making of Humanity*. Cambridge: Cambridge University Press, 1999.

Ricoeur, Paul. "The Model of the Text: Meaningful Action Considered as a Text." *Social Research* 38 (1971): 529–62.

Robbins, Joel. *Becoming Sinners: Christianity and Moral Torment in a Papua New Guinea Society*. Berkeley: University of California Press, 2004.

– "Monism, Pluralism and the Structure of Value Relations: A Dumontian Contribution to the Contemporary Study of Value." *Hau* 3, no. 1 (2013): 99–115.

– "Dumont's Hierarchical Dynamism: Christianity and Individualism Revisited." *Hau: Journal of Ethnographic Theory* 5, no. 1 (2015): 173–95.

– "What Is the Matter with Transcendence? On the Place of Religion in the New Anthropology of Ethics (with commentary)." *Journal of the Royal Anthropological Institute* 22, no. 4 (2016): 757–808.

– *Theology and the Anthropology of Christian Life*. Oxford: Oxford University Press, 2020.

Rorty, Richard. *Philosophy and the Mirror of Nature*. Princeton, NJ: Princeton University Press, 1980.

Ruel, Malcolm. "Christians as Believers." In *Religious Organization and Religious Experience*, edited by John Davis. London: Academic Press, 1982. Reprinted in M. Lambek, ed., *A Reader in the Anthropology of Religion*. 2nd ed. Malden, MA: Wiley-Blackwell, 2008.

Ryle, Gilbert. *The Concept of Mind*. Chicago: University of Chicago Press, 1949.

– *Dilemmas (Tarner Lectures of 1953)*. Cambridge: Cambridge University Press, 1962.

– *Collected Papers, Vol. 2: Collected Essays 1929–1968*. London: Hutchinson, 1971.

Sahlins, Marshall. "The Original Political Society." *Hau: Journal of Ethnographic Theory* 7, no. 2 (2017): 91–128.

Scarry, Elaine. "On Beauty and Being Just." Tanner Lectures on Human Values, delivered at Yale University, New Haven, CT, 1998. (Published by Princeton University Press, Princeton, NJ, 2001.)

Schutz, Alfred. "The Well-Informed Citizen: An Essay on the Social Distribution of Knowledge." In *Collected Papers*, edited by Alfred Schutz, vol. 2. The Hague: Martinus Nijhoff, 1964.

Segal, Hanna. *Introduction to the Work of Melanie Klein*. London: Hogarth Press, 1982.

Selka, Stephen. "Demons and Money." In *Spirited Things: The Work of "Possession" in Afro-Atlantic Religions*, edited by Paul Christopher Johnson, 155–75. Chicago: University of Chicago Press, 2014.

Sidnell, Jack. *Talk and Practical Epistemology: The Social Life of Knowledge in a Caribbean Community*. Amsterdam: John Benjamins, 2005.

– "Ethical Projects, or How to Bring about a Way of Life." Unpublished paper.

Spillius, Elizabeth, and E. O'Shaughnessy, eds. *The Writings of Melanie Klein*, vols I–IV. London: Hogarth Press, 1984.

– *Projective Identification*. London: Routledge, 2012.

Stallybrass, Peter, and Allon White. *The Politics and Poetics of Transgression*. Ithaca, NY: Cornell University Press, 1986.

Stern, Stanley. "My Experience of Analysis with Loewald." *The Psychoanalytic Quarterly* LXXVIII, no. 4 (2009): 1013–31.

Stoler, Ann Laura. *Duress: Imperial Durabilities in Our Times*. Durham, NC: Duke University Press, 2016.

Strathern, Marilyn. "An Awkward Relationship: The Case of Feminism and Anthropology." *Signs* 12, no. 2, Reconstructing the Academy (Winter 1987): 276–92.

Tambiah, Stanley. *Culture, Thought, and Social Action*. Cambridge, MA: Harvard University Press, 1985.

Tanner, Kathryn. "Theology and Cultural Contest in the University." In *Religious Studies, Theology, and the University: Conflicting Maps, Changing*

Terrain, edited by L.E. Cady and D. Brown, 199–212. Albany: State University of New York Press, 2002.

Taylor, Anne-Christine. "Distinguishing Ontologies: Comment on Lloyd, G.E.R. 2012. *Being, Humanity, and Understanding.*" *HAU: Journal of Ethnographic Theory* 3, no. 1 (2013): 201–4.

Tehindrazanarivelo, Emmanuel. "Fieldwork: The Dance of Power." *Anthropology and Humanism* 22, no. 1 (1997): 54–6. Special issue edited by Sandra Bamford and Joel Robbins.

Thompson, Michael. *Life and Action.* Cambridge, MA: Harvard University Press, 2012.

Turner, Victor. *The Ritual Process.* Chicago: Aldine, 1969.

Verdery, Katherine. *My Life as a Spy: Investigations in a Secret Police File.* Durham, NC: Duke University Press, 2018.

Viveiros de Castro, Eduardo. "The Relative Native." *Hau: Journal of Ethnographic Theory* 3, no. 3 (2013): 473–502.

– *Cannibal Metaphysics.* Translated by Peter Skafish. Minneapolis. MN: Univocal Publishing, 2014.

Waldenfels, Bernhard. *Phenomenology of the Alien.* Evanston, IL: Northwestern University Press, 2011.

Wentzer, Thomas Schwarz. "'I Have Seen Königsberg Burning': Philosophical Anthropology and the Responsiveness of Historical Experience." *Anthropological Theory* 14, no. 1 (2014): 27–48.

Werbner, Richard. *Divination's Grasp: African Encounters with the Almost Said.* Bloomington: Indiana University Press, 2015.

Whitehead, Alfred North. *Science and the Modern World.* New York: Palgrave Macmillan, 1925.

Williams, Bernard. "Ethical Consistency" and "Consistency and Realism." In his *Problems of the Self,* 166–86, and 187–204. Cambridge: Cambridge University Press, 1973.

– *Ethics and the Limits of Philosophy.* London: Fontana, 1985.

– *Shame and Necessity.* Berkeley: University of California Press, 1993.

Williams, Raymond. *Keywords: A Vocabulary of Culture and Society.* London: Fontana, 1976.

Williams, Rowan (former Archbishop of Canterbury). "The Theology of Personhood: A Study of the Thought of Christos Yannaras." *Sobornost* 6 (1972): 415–30.

Winnicott, D.W. *Playing and Reality.* London: Routledge, 1991.

Witherspoon, Gary. *Language and Art in the Navajo Universe.* Ann Arbor: University of Michigan Press, 1977.

Wittgenstein, Ludwig. *Tractatus Logico-Philosophicus*. Translated by D.F. Pears and B.F. McGuinness. London: Routledge, 1961 [1922].

– *Philosophical Investigations*. Translated by G.E.M. Anscombe. 3rd ed. Englewood Cliffs, NJ: Prentice Hall, 2000 [1953].

– *The Mythology in Our Language: Remarks on Frazer's Golden Bough*. Edited by Stephan Palmié and Giovanni da Col; translated by Stephan Palmié. Chicago: Hau Books, 2020 [1967].

Zaidman, Louise Bruit, and Pauline Schmitt Pantel. *Religion in the Ancient Greek City*. Translated by Paul Cartledge. Cambridge: University of Cambridge Press, 1992.

Zweig, Stefan. *The Royal Game (Schachnovelle, Chess Story): The Royal Game and Other Stories*. New York: E.P. Dutton, 1981 [1941].

Commentators

Jonathan Lear is the John U. Nef Distinguished Service Professor at the Committee on Social Thought and in the Department of Philosophy at the University of Chicago. He trained in philosophy at the University of Cambridge and the Rockefeller University, where he received his PhD in 1978. He works primarily on philosophical conceptions of the human psyche from Socrates to the present and also trained as a psychoanalyst at the Western New England Institute for Psychoanalysis. He is a recipient of the Andrew W. Mellon Foundation Distinguished Achievement Award. In 2014, he was appointed the Roman Family Director of the Neubauer Collegium for Culture and Society and continues in that role currently. He is a Fellow of the American Academy of Arts and Sciences and a Member of the American Philosophical Society.

Sherry B. Ortner is a Distinguished Research Professor of Anthropology at UCLA. She received her AB from Bryn Mawr College and her MA and PhD from the University of Chicago, and she has taught at Sarah Lawrence College; the University of Michigan; the University of California, Berkeley; and Columbia University. She has been the recipient of numerous grants, fellowships, and awards, including those from the National Science Foundation, the Guggenheim Foundation, the National Endowment for the Humanities, and the John D. and Catherine T. MacArthur Foundation. Her book *Life and Death on Mt. Everest* was awarded the J.I. Staley Prize for the best anthropology book of 2004. She has been elected to the American Academy of Arts and Sciences and has been awarded the Retzius Medal of the Society for Anthropology and Geography of Sweden.

Joel Robbins is the Sigrid Rausing Professor of Social Anthropology at the University of Cambridge and a Fellow at Trinity College. He earned his PhD from the University of Virginia in 1998 and has published works on the anthropology of Papua New Guinea, anthropological theory, the anthropology of Christianity, religious change, the anthropology of ethics and morals, and the anthropology of value. Ethnographically, he is known for his work with the Urapmin people. His book *Becoming Sinners: Christianity and Moral Torment in a Papua New Guinea Society* was awarded the J.I. Staley Prize by the School for Advanced Research in 2011. His most recent book is *Theology and the Anthropology of Christian Life*.

Index

Misak, Cheryl, 4n11
mistakes. *See* category mistakes;
  errors
monism, 48, 112–13, 120, 123, 129
morality: and games, 66; moral
  thought, 29; word, 26
Motta, Marco, 128n2
mourning, x, 75–7, 83, 90–1, 93–4
Mulhall, Stephen, 33n96, 35, 71
Mulidy, 17, 69
Munn, Nancy, 111
Murdoch, Iris, 51n145
Myerhoff, Barbara, 124n26

Napolitano, Valentina, 42n119
Narboux, Jean-Philippe, 67n12
nature/culture problem:
  conceptual dilemma of, 24,
  34, 48; as existential, 115; and
  incommensurability, 120, 129;
  and mind/body problem,
  11n30; Roy Rappaport
  on, 52n146
Nehamas, Alexander, 4n9, 35
Nietzsche, Friedrich, 23n61,
  28n81, 129n5
Nuttall, Mark, 26n71

Obeyesekere, Gananath, 89n8
Orsi, Robert, 20n55,
  41n114, 131
Ortiz, Alfonso, 122n19
Ortner, Sherry, 3n5, 4n9,
  26n74, 106. *See also "Another
  Description: Serious Games"*
  (55–61 passim); *"On Games:
  A Response to Sherry Ortner"*
  (62–71 passim)
O'Shaughnessy, E., 78n4

Pandolfo, Stefania, 89n8
Parker, Robert, 40n113
personification, 41, 44
philosophy: alternative traditions,
  6n16; contrasted with
  anthropology, 2–7, 29n85,
  52; as description, 5n14; and
  self-critique, 47, 83–5, 100;
  therapeutic task, 2
phronesis, 20
pluralism, 112–13, 123, 129
Pope, Alexander, 46n130, 52n147
posthuman, 2n3
Pouillon, Jean, 45n127
practice, theory, 56, 64
Premawardhana, Devaka, 122n19
pretence, 67–8
psychoanalytic perspective, 78–9,
  87–9, 91n12, 93n22, 118
putting things under description:
  and anthropological practice,
  4–6, 17–18, 37, 51, 103, 119–20,
  128; and conceptual mistakes,
  38n109; holding to, 32; and
  judgment, 118; as moral task,
  19n50; Salim's attempts at, 30;
  and theories of games, 66, 70;
  and values, 110

Qur'an, 14, 15, 43

Radin, Paul, 6n16
Rappaport, Roy, 2n3, 5n13, 46,
  49n141, 52n146, 69n19, 123
rationality, 23n60, 28, 29n85, 49–50,
  115, 129; reason and
  judgment, 38
reality, difficulty of, 21, 80–4,
  93–6, 100